Notes from
Anoth

Pete Cross was born in Redruth in 1962 and grew up in Truro. He gained an honours degree from Bath Academy of Art, then spent the following fifteen years working in London publishing houses and travelling. On returning to Cornwall at the beginning of the new millennium, he began writing a column for *Cornwall Today*, which soon became known as *Backalong*. An anthology of these columns, *Notes from a Cornish Shed*, was published at the end of 2013. His children's book, *Shadows in the Sky*, was published in 2007 to widespread acclaim, and won the *Waterstones Holyer an Gof Special Prize*.

He lives in an old miner's cottage on the north Cornish coast with his wife, twin boys, and an assortment of chickens and geese.

Also by Pete Cross

Shadows in the Sky
Notes from a Cornish Shed

Praise for
Notes from a Cornish Shed:

'All written with a smile on his face, Pete's
tales are a joy to read.' *Kernow King*

'Pete Cross's books are delightful – he has a poetic
and wry take on life and all he observes.'
Alison Barrow, Transworld Publishing

'… Pete Cross can be relied on to give us an
insightful and entertaining vision of living in
Cornwall today.'
Ann Kelley, author of *The Bower Bird*

'…it's a cracking good read.' *Cornish Guardian*

Notes from a Cornish Shed: Another Shedload

Another choice selection of
Pete Cross' *Backalong* columns
from *Cornwall Today* magazine

ONE INCH
CAPACITY

First published in Great Britain in 2017 by
One Inch Capacity
www.oneinchcapacity.co.uk

Text © Pete Cross 2017
Design © One Inch Capacity 2017

ISBN 978-0-9926451-2-0

A catalogue record for this book is available from the British Library.

Jacket design by in©

Jacket photography by marekp.co.uk

Cornwall Today logo reproduced by kind permission of
Cornwall and Devon Media

Printed and bound in Cornwall by TJ International, Padstow

For Liz Cross

CONTENTS

Introduction

Welcome!

Here we go then: a shedload more *Backalongs*. Volume one seemed to go down all right, so it was only a matter of time until the idea of a second collection began to stir. I spent some time trawling through the archive, and against all the odds, found that therein lay a reasonable seam of new material. When I say *new*, I obviously mean, well, *old*. As with volume one I've plucked them out, brushed them off, given them a light edit, and 'ere ye go.

The first volume provoked some interesting responses. People who like to read at bedtime reported uncomfortable occasions when they've woken up only to be confronted by me gurning at them from their bedside table. That huge cover photo on volume one wasn't my idea, I swear. You may have noticed that we've gone for a smaller photo this time around, partly to minimise this potential trauma. You're welcome.

Someone I don't know that well told me that she found volume one a disconcerting experience since it made her feel 'like a stalker'. I don't know what to do about this. Surely it's the job of any columnist to express an opinion, and, by definition, this means put something of themselves into it. Just how much they reveal is entirely up to the individual. Sure, I've enjoyed getting a few things off my chest over the years, but my monthly *Backalong* column is usually – no – *always*, tongue-in-cheek, and not to be taken too seriously. I mean, out of all the columns in this volume, the one that probably provoked the most comment was the one in which I lament the loss of a flip-flop. No, it still hasn't turned up, since you ask.

I do always hope that what I say will strike a chord or prompt an approving nod, or even, on occasion, a chuckle from the reader. But that's all. I deliberately restrain myself from letting my inner demons run away with me, or from getting carried away about politics, because *a)* I'd probably end up offending someone (and we wouldn't want that), and *b)* I'd be way out of my depth. Generally, I've had a lovely response from people. If I hadn't, the thing in your hand wouldn't exist.

Most worryingly, my friend Andy told me that he really enjoyed volume one, but then spoiled it all by elaborating on one of the reasons. Apparently reading an average *Backalong* column takes him exactly the same amount of time as his daily expurgation. Yep, it appears that this creative endeavour over which I toil monthly is perfectly synchronised with a different type of creative endeavour: one over which a tall, bald man toils daily. Eeww.

I didn't quite know how to respond to this cheerful proclamation – any writer will tell you that it's nice to receive positive comments – but this really is stretching things. Andy seemed to be under the impression that his news would come as no surprise to me, as if I might already have been aware of a small but significant toilet demographic, and that he was merely confirming things. As if it was quite conceivable that I'd modified the duration of my *Backalong* column accordingly.

9

Well thanks for the thought Andy, but I can assure you that I didn't plan it that way. To be honest, the only positive I've managed to take from your bathroom declaration is to make a mental note to never lend you any books.

As part of the process of compiling this second collection, I've re-read every column I've ever written. There's plenty that hasn't changed: people are still walking around Cornwall in January wearing shorts and flip-flops, still living the dream, still as keen as ever to prove to themselves that they're living somewhere subtropical (despite the, er, *cold weather*). Ludicrously neat logs remain stacked wherever people spot a likely looking alcove, still showing no sign of ever being set light to (in fact you now don't even have to bother with the inconvenience of actual logs. You can get wallpaper with them on. Yes, as if 'display logs' weren't nutty enough – now you've got trompe l'oeil ones. You couldn't make it up). Oh, and opera fans still seem inexplicably adamant that every person in the known universe would love opera if only the poor dears could just go to one.

But it's the columns that remind us of certain moments in time that I find the most interesting: that amazing first day of the Olympic torch's journey through Cornwall...the floods of '13-14...the euphoria of the Cornish chough's natural return. And then there's *Poldark*. It's easy to forget how charged the atmosphere was, prior to the first episode of the new version in 2015. Remember all that sucking of teeth, and sideways glancing, and people saying 'Crikey that's risky isn't it, I mean they'll never find another Robin Ellis, let alone an Angharad

Rees'. But since the new incarnation began, it's taken the world by storm, and had a tangible effect in Cornwall. Exactly like it did in the seventies. And it's provided me with a fertile source of *Backalong* material. As you'll see in the pages that follow, when it comes to *Poldark*, I haven't held back.

Anyway that's enough introduction, or there won't be any room left for the book. Finally, I'd just like to thank Kirstie, esteemed editor of *Cornwall Today* magazine. Several editors have come and gone in the years I've been writing *Backalong*, but she's been running the show at *CT* for quite some time now. She's always professional, helpful, and, above all, great fun. That might sound like grovelling, but honestly, she's been good to me, and she didn't have to be. Plus, she's practically never told me to alter an article because I'm being silly. Which means either I'm doing it right, or she's as daft as me.

And she's definitely not daft.

National minority

2014

T hings started normally enough when I was roused from sleep by the alarm clock radio. But lying there, I could have sworn that I heard John Humphreys saying something about Cornwall.

"Flippin' *Jamaica Inn* again," I mumbled, drifting momentarily back to sleep, vaguely recalling that the final episode had aired the previous evening. They hadn't stopped talking about *Joss Merlyn-gate* in the media for the past three days, due to the fact that they'd had such problems with the sound quality. Personally I thought they'd had a pretty good stab at the book, and the accents weren't nearly as bad as one has come to expect from these things. This is despite the fact that Joss was supposed to be seven feet tall, the Vicar of Altarnun an albino, and there's no way Mary should have gamely succumbed to Jem's charms upstairs in the tavern after Launceston Market. And I don't recall Daphne du Maurier using dreadful Americanisms like 'we're gonna do jail-time', or going on about people getting 'busted'. And they definitely didn't indulge in a rather protracted and ludicrous wild-west-style gunfight climax at the summit of Rough Tor in the book.

But that's just my opinion, probably tainted because I love the book, and am more than a tad overprotective towards it.

All in all I thought the disappointingly short but still very menacing actor who played Joss did well. However the director who told him that his style of constant whispering-through-gritted teeth was uniquely effective, should definitely not be let near a big budget BBC adaptation any time soon, at least not as long as this viewer is forking out £145 a year for a licence.

Anyway. Humphreys raised his voice slightly and jolted me back to life. Strewth, I thought. This was the BBC's flagship *national* news radio station, and Humphreys *was* talking about Cornwall. But not a word about Jamaica Inn. It seemed that the headline, first thing in the morning of the 24th of April, was that the Cornish had just been 'recognised as a national minority group'. And then there was Danny Alexander, no less, saying, "Cornish people have a proud history and a distinct identity. I am delighted that we have been able to officially recognise this and afford the Cornish people the same status as other minorities in the UK". Buzzwords were bandied about: 'combating discrimination, promoting equality and preserving and developing the culture and identity of national minorities…distinctiveness of the Cornish…aims of the framework convention…' It was as if I was dreaming, and yet I was wide awake now.

I lay there, wide-eyed. Incredible, I thought. So we're a national minority. Now, today. After all this time. I couldn't believe it. All these years of waiting. All that work. I got dressed, still trying to take in the news. I went downstairs to the pandemonium that is breakfast-time with two six-year-olds (you will have gathered that I'm not the earliest riser in our house. In fact I'm very much the latest). I put the kettle on and waited for the noise level to drop below that of, well, two six-year-olds shouting at each other and banging things, which I know from past experience happens about every forty seconds when both twins take a mouthful of Superhoops at exactly the same moment.

I turned to the missus and said, "Have you heard? About the national minority status thing?"

She turned to me with intense eyes, and replied, "I know. Amazing".

"I just can't take it in. This is going to be huge."

"Yep," she said. "National minority. Brilliant." She paused for a moment or two, then said, "Um, what does it mean exactly? I mean, *really*?"

I thought for a bit, took a deep breath, and considered my reply. "I've no idea," I said.

Life of Brian

2017

I n 1979, Monty Python's *Life of Brian* was released. Not that I went to see it. No-one did.

Not in Cornwall anyway. Regularly voted funniest British film of all time, it was banned in our county (and several other places throughout the UK and beyond). A film that we now recognise as a hilarious satire on organised religion was considered so profane, so *blasphemous*, that it was actually withheld from the public lest we...well, I don't really know what was supposed to happen to us if we watched it. To be honest, if any person's faith was ever so vulnerable as to be jeopardised by this bit of affectionate mockery, then the film was probably providing them with a useful service.

It seems odd now, but banning *Life of Brian* didn't seem all that surprising at the time. When I recall Cornwall in the seventies, in many respects it was a grey sort of place – a place where there wasn't even a nightclub to go to when the Truro pubs called time on a Saturday night. Such was the lingering grip of our rural Methodist tradition. Our aspirations were more limited then. Never mind the Eden Project – St Agnes Model Village was an exciting afternoon out. We lived with it, just as we'd lived with the three-day week and the resigned acceptance of a small glass of concentrated orange juice as a restaurant starter. So when the 'powers that be' decided that we should not be allowed to watch the new Monty Python film, we sighed a collective Cornish sigh, and mumbled a sad but submissive, "Ah well".

Of course, during the ensuing months and years we all got to see it, either on video or by travelling to less, er, *fundamentalist* places. I finally found out what all the fuss was about in 1981, a full two years after *Life of Brian*'s release. I was spending a few days in London with fellow Falmouth School of Art students, and noticed that it was showing in a cinema near our digs. Now was my chance! My friends were too busy indulging in the more traditional hedonistic pursuits of the art student, but I saw this as a golden opportunity, so I ducked out and went on my own. I suppose it was my own act of defiance – indulging in clandestine activity that was *illegal* in my home county! Certainly something to tell everyone about when I got back over the Tamar. "Pete's seen *Life of Brian*!" they'd say, "He went to *London!*"

The funny thing is, when I finally got to see Monty Python's masterpiece, I was disappointed. By the time I took my seat and the lights dimmed, I'd convinced myself that it was going to change my life. It didn't. After two years of mounting anticipation, it couldn't possibly live up to my expectations.

I've no idea how many times I've seen it, or bits of it, since that evening. And of course like most people, I love it now. I see it as a group of very funny men mercilessly poking fun at all kinds of pomposity, in a very British sort of way. Everyone can quote at least a line from *Life of Brian,* and certainly whistle

Eric Idle's closing song. My wife delights in reciting entire scenes verbatim.

Everything's different now. The Monty Python team have gone from establishment-smashing surrealists to lovable national treasures. 'Pythonesque' is in the Oxford English Dictionary. Banning *Life of Brian* is seen as an ill-informed, kneejerk overreaction from, well, another century. In 2014, thirty-five years after its release, the *Plaza* in Truro finally showed it for the first time. The UK's foremost film critic Mark Kermode was there to host not one, but two consecutive evenings. Its screening was a highly significant moment, made all the more poignant for me by the fact that it was shown at the very cinema where I'd have watched it in 1979.

What a different world, and what a different Cornwall.

Poldark

2014

S o, a brand new adaptation of the *Poldark* books is only months away. It's a BBC job – big name cast, lavish production, all the trimmings. The tension is palpable. I for one can't wait.

It's hard to imagine, for those who weren't living in Cornwall at the time, how significant the original series in the seventies was. It seemed as if the whole world was enthralled by the shenanigans based around an 18th century west Cornwall mining family, and Robin Ellis and Angharad Rees understandably became household names. Fifteen million people used to tune in on Sunday nights, and vicars throughout Cornwall famously had to reschedule Sunday evening services due to dwindling congregations. We all adored it.

Cornwall benefitted demonstrably too. I remember how many more holidaymakers the series attracted. I can clearly recall a car pulling up in Truro circa 1977, the driver winding down his car window to ask, "Ey oop, can you tell us the way t't *Poldark* country?" *Poldark*'s effect on Cornwall was like that of *Doc Martin* now, multiplied by about a million.

There's still so much love for the original seventies series that the naysayers are already damning the BBC's new project:

'If it ain't broke, don't fix it…Angharad Rees was the only true Demelza…no-one will ever match the chemistry between her and Robin…' My wife's one of them.

I suppose the last attempt to resurrect *Poldark* on TV, the doomed ITV series of 1996, didn't help. But I for one am very excited about the new adaptation. The original series was amazing, but it was the seventies. The sets, dare I say it, were a bit creaky. Some of the accents were very bad indeed. Angharad Rees completely owned the role of Demelza and we loved her, but she must have gone to that strange place somewhere between Bristol and Norfolk to learn her accent. It was certainly a considerable distance from Illogan.

Let's face it, in the seventies we'd have watched anything. You could have put paint drying on BBC1 on Sunday night and the next morning we'd all have been discussing it around whatever the 1976 equivalent of the water cooler was. Remember *The Brothers*, that unforgettable saga based within a London-based road-haulage business? Seven series it ran for. That was then. We're in the 21st century now, the age of *Breaking Bad* and *Broadchurch*. This new *Poldark* adaptation should be dark, thrilling and authentic, an altogether different animal. It is time. At least I'm willing to hope so.

As for the casting, naysayers are already claiming that Aidan Turner is the wrong choice to don the leather coat and breeches to play the complex, damaged, brooding, eponymous hero. To me he looks perfect. At least give the man a chance. I reckon the casting team's made some great choices. They've got Kneehigh's Tristan Sturrock to play Zacky Martin, and he

19

definitely knows his way around a Cornish accent. Jud and Prudie are arguably the biggest shoes to fill. They were both a highlight of the seventies series due to the actors' masterly dialect, which they mercilessly exploited to comic effect. But Phil Davis and Beatie Edney must be two of the safest pairs of hands in the business, so it will be interesting to see how they play it. And whoever came up with the idea of asking Robin Ellis to play a small part is a genius. Of course we all know that all eyes will be on Demelza, particularly in the crucial "*Oh Ross*" scene (in fact this one moment could make or break the entire thing).

There are so many reasons we should be giving it a chance. It should definitely bring a lot of people to Cornwall, and if they're interested in exploring our awe-inspiring, and often overlooked, mining history, then bring it on.

Above all, to write off the new adaptation before it's even started is an insult to the memory of a great writer. Winston Graham's sublime series of books envelops you in a completely convincing world full of well-crafted, complex characters about whom you really care. So I say roll on episode one.

Now all I've got to do is persuade the missus to watch it with me.

The way it is

2013

I think I'm onto something. I've spent all these years getting all het up about it, and the fog's finally lifted.

For over thirteen years I've beavered away in the house and garden – hacking brambles back, yanking out weeds, planting things, raking leaves, cutting back hedges, unblocking drains, touching up, rewiring, repointing cracks, scrubbing and repainting previously unnoticed damp patches...

All standard stuff for a 250-year-old cottage with an acre of land. Nothing special, just routine maintenance. But it takes up a lot of time. It's got to the point that when asked what I do with my spare time, I simply find myself saying "Well, I just work on the house and garden". But I've been working away all these years with this vague sense that I'm working, well, *towards something*. A sense that somehow, someday, it will end. Or at least slow down enough for me to occasionally do other things. I've always had this innate feeling that if I keep on going, I'll reach a kind of destination. Perfection, even. I've been assuming that on some undefined date somewhere in the future, it will suddenly hit me: *I've done it*. I've arrived. The place will be entirely resolved. The garden will look finished, and all I'll ever have to do now is a bit of basic maintenance. And inside the house, the damp patches will all have been dealt with, and the draughts will all be gone, and all the taps will have stopped dripping forever, and every single one of the floorboards will have stopped squeaking. I will have achieved a kind of domestic nirvana. It will finally be like living in a modern house, with a normal, manageable garden that is mostly lawn.

And so the years have passed. And the truth is, I've never reached anything approaching nirvana. Quite the opposite. I still spend every available hour sorting the place out. In fact it's probably more work than ever, due to the fact that it's only stopped raining on one occasion in the past four years (one day in March 2012, I think it was, for a couple of hours in the late afternoon). Like a lot of people, especially in Cornwall, I've ended up prey to the relentless, depressing sensation that my world and everything in it is slowly, steadily, *dampening*.

But now, out of the blue, the most spectacular truth has revealed itself to me. And it's making a big difference. I've realised: *it doesn't end*. Not ever. And it's not supposed to. And do you know what? That's OK. I've come to terms with it. Living in an old Cornish house with a bit of land shouldn't be, and never has been, about aiming for a goal. True enlightenment lies in the acceptance that it's ongoing. A project. To seek more is simply unrealistic. I know that even if I put my heart and soul into repointing the cracked crazy paving, and succeeded in removing every inch of ivy root from the soil, something else would come along to vex me just as badly. The ivy lurking in my old Cornish hedges will always be invading the garden. The place is always going to be a bit scruffy. Old places just are. It's part of their charm. When you get inside a vintage car that's been lovingly restored to showroom condition it's very impressive. But it's much more satisfying to get into an old car with authentically cracked leather seats, and run your fingers along the scuff marks on the walnut trim, because every one has a story to tell. You can't buy character like that.

I may be living in a state of perpetual crisis management, but that's just life in an old place. It's the price you pay for living somewhere with history, and character, and charm. I used to be no better than those poor people you see on documentaries, spending unaffordable amounts of money on surgical enhancement of various bits of their body and face in an attempt to perfect themselves. That way lies obsession and madness. Enjoy what you've got, do what you can, and admit that the pursuit of perfection is simply not realistic. That's just the way it is.

Crimp

2013

There's hell up down the Lizard. I've always been careful about mentioning the word *pasty* in this column, on account of it being, well, a bit of a cliché, and the fact that I'd be risking ridicule for bringing up such an obvious subject in a Cornish magazine. But once in a while you get the calling. This is something that needs saying. It's political, even.

Now Ann, of the eponymous pasty emporium in Lizard Village, is, in my opinion, purveyor of the finest pasties commercially available to a Cornishperson (and I have committed the best part of fifty years to researching the subject). Whenever I've ventured down that way for an RSPB chough nest-watch shift, I've stopped at Ann's. In fact on one occasion on a night shift I enjoyed one in the afternoon and another, cold, after dark. Not that I'd ever recommend a pasty for consecutive meals, no matter how tasty. That's hardcore, and even I'm not that Cornish. I got caught without my trusty blister pack of *Rennies* once and regretted it. Never made that mistake again.

Anyway, back to Ann. Her ingredients are chopped super fine, and perfectly seasoned. The pastry has this mythical elastic quality that you have to experience to believe, as if she adds half a teaspoon of latex to the mix. Hmm...tasty, lardy latex. I've asked her how she does it and I got little back, sensible woman. As for the insides, she of course sticks to the four ingredients: beef skirt, teddies, turnip, onion, bit o' seasoning. Not rocket science, yet surprisingly easy to get wrong. Ann doesn't get it wrong. She's been doing it a while. She's got history. She still uses the rolling pin her grandmother used to make pasties. Hell, her mother wrote books on the subject. Ann crimps 'em on the top, like most people. My family certainly always has. Well, not right on top, thinking about it. More sort of, three quarters. Wherever it ends up, really. Three quarters is usually the natural place they do end up when you start crimpin'.

And there, as they say, lies the rub. For crimping them beauties on top these days is a sin, an offence so heinous that it renders the whole thing *not Cornish*. The *Pasty Police* declare that (among a long list of other criteria), a pasty must be crimped *along the side*, so that the whole thing forms a sort of 'D' shape. It can't even be a three quarter crimp. And so, despite the fact that Ann's pasties are made in deepest Cornwall, by a Cornish grandmother, who knows all about it, her pasties ent Cornish. What strange times we do live in.

To give it its correct name, the *Cornish Pasty Association* was formed with doubtless honourable intentions to prevent they beggars upcountry and beyond coming up with all sorts of rubbish and calling it a Cornish pasty. Fair enough. But the reality is that when you start to draw up a list of conditions that will define what makes a pasty 'Cornish', some very odd things start to happen.

Course, we Cornish couldn't care less if the pasty in our hand is prefixed by a certain adjective or not. We're too discerning. We're always perfectly aware of a pasty's provenance, long before we pick it up and sniff it. It's either been made by someone we know, or come from a shop we know. So none of this rubbish really matters to us. And in all the years I lived away from Cornwall, if I ever came near any kind of pasty, I'd view it with great suspicion. Any Cornishperson would. It's in our genes. For this reason, I'm not really qualified to adjudicate on how our sacred dish should be represented upcountry. And it's definitely well outside my frame of reference to comprehend the economic necessity for a regulatory body to oversee the definition of 'Cornish' pasty.

All I know is, Ann's pasties are 'ansum. To declare that they are un-Cornish is, well, just plain bonkers.

Olympics

2012

R emember the day London won its Olympic bid? For the next fortnight, every news bulletin seemed to feature footage of Lord Seb Coe and Dame Kelly Holmes jumping up and down in the fountain in Trafalgar Square, or wherever it was, while thwarted Parisians grumbled under their breath: *"They can keep their stupeed Olympics – We nevair wanted them anyway"*. Seems like yesterday, and yet now they are almost upon us.

My enthusiasm for the Games has waxed and waned and waxed again over the years. In phase one, all those years ago, I met the news with uncharacteristic enthusiasm, and looked forward to the summer of 2012 when my whole family would go and stay with my brother, who lives a stone's throw from the Olympic village. I calculated that, at four-and-a-half, my twin boys would be just the right age for the experience to become their first significant memory. And what a memory. The Olympic Games, in their own capital city, and they would be there, to see it, first hand, live! It would be amazing!

And then we applied for tickets. The range of events and seat options seemed limitless. Yet we could find no information about either the number of seats in each category, nor where they were. We surmised that a £20 seat would be considerably further back than a £300 one, but beyond that we had no idea what exactly it was that we were applying for. Entering the lottery for tickets, we felt as informed as someone betting on a horse in the Grand National, knowing nothing about the horse, nor indeed whether it was even a horse. It might have been a monkey.

Avoiding any of the conventionally popular events, we tactically put in for over £700 worth of tickets, right across the board. And got nothing. Neither did my brother, who'd been enthusiastically observing the erection of the Olympic complex on his doorstep, telling visitors all about it, not to mention paying 38p per week *Olympic Council Tax Levy* for the previous few years and for an indefinite number of years to come.

Crestfallen, and with a bad taste in my mouth, I entered phase two. Resigned cynicism. Much more *me*, to be honest. They 'released' some more tickets, and we were patronisingly informed of 'another chance for unsuccessful applicants to apply for tickets for their favourite events'. But unless left-handed outdoor ping pong was your secret passion, the list of remaining available events held scant interest. The entirely predictable multi billion-pound overspend during what was turning out to be the worst recession for at least a generation didn't help my mood either. Flipping Olympics. They should've gone to France.

But then out of the blue, I entered phase three, and at least partially, regained my enthusiasm. My missus, along with 7,999 other deserving souls, was to be a torchbearer on May 19, the very first day of its circuitous 70-day journey from Land's

End to London. This could be good, I thought. My wife following in the footsteps of Prometheus! Fleetingly, my inner Cornish nationalist took umbrage that Cornwall was only to get the torch for one day out of 70. This couldn't be right. Surely Lord Coe of all people knows we're not just another county, but a proud Celtic nation?

But then I looked at a map, and, bearing in mind that the gold cheese grater thingy has to also pass through 46 English counties, and Wales, Scotland and Ireland, not to mention various islands, we were probably doing OK out of the deal. We are, after all, long and thin, and if the aim was for the torch to travel 'within ten miles of 95 per cent of people in the UK', fair enough. Damn shame it couldn't have started on Bryher though. That would've been nice.

So it turns out I'm going to get in on the action after all. Or at least my wife is, which is sort of the same. Thank you, Olympics. At least my boys will see their mum taking part in a tiny piece of history. Even if we are reduced to watching Tom Daley win his medal from a sofa in Goon Gumpas.

Launceston

2014

M *ouse hole.*
No, of course: *Mouzle*. There can't be a person in the developed world that doesn't know that. Praa Sands? *Pray* Sands. When my pals and I used to cycle along the lanes around Truro as kids, we'd often go through the tiny hamlet of Idless. We always pronounced it *Eedless*. And for St Columb, we always said *St Culumb*. No-one ever told us why.

You pick these things up pretty quickly, if you don't want to look a fool. To wrongly pronounce a place name has always been one of the most obvious pitfalls for the newcomer, or visitor. This applies wherever you are in the world. We've all done it. At best it causes a sideways glance. At worst, outright contempt.

In Cornwall, the opportunity to scoff at those unwittingly getting it 'wrong' seems to present itself on a regular basis. Within the past fortnight, I've heard 'Illogan' pronounced 'Ill-log-an' and also 'Ill-low-gan', even though any idiot knows it's 'Ill-lug-an' (well, any idiot within a two mile radius of Illogan anyway). Not long ago we had a friend staying who'd just visited Marazion. Hilariously he pronounced the name with the stress on the second syllable, instead of the third! 'Ma-RAZ-eeyun.' Imagine! I can't pretend that my wife and I didn't enjoy the puerile thrill of letting someone carry on talking, while unknowingly making a bit of a twit of themselves.

But wait a minute. Let's not be too hasty here. I mean, who sets these rules exactly? Your average place name comes with a lot of history – most places have been through dozens of versions, over hundreds of years, before arriving at what we deem to be some sort of conclusion. Who's to say that our pronunciation of these names is a final decision? Who declared closure? A few years ago someone started pronouncing the word 'homage' in its original, French, posh-sounding 'om-arj' form, instead of 'hom-idge'. It caught on, and suddenly everyone's doing it.

Just look at Launceston. No, not our one. The Australian one. Rather laughably to our Cornish ear, Tasmanians pronounce the name with the full three syllables. Yep, *Lawn-sess-tun*. I was in Lawn-sess-tun, Tasmania a few years ago, and got chatting to a friendly looking native. I naively assumed that this lady might like to hear how we pronounce the Cornish town of the same name (not the hardcore, locals-only 'Laans'n', you understand. Just our everyday 'Lawns-tun'). The Tasmanian looked at me with a disdain that chills me to this day, and said something along the lines of "Not only is that a stupid way to pronounce what is plainly a three-syllable word, but I doubt there is another town with the same name in the world, let alone in the very place you claim to come from". Our two-syllable Launceston was as ridiculous to her as her three-syllable one is to us. I didn't dare try to explain that *her* Launceston was actually named after our Cornish one. And so

31

I spent a day and a night in Lawn-sess-tun, Tasmania, the whole time feeling a bit superior, but at the same time, slightly annoyed.

But who am I to dictate that the Tasmanians have got it wrong? Lawn-sess-tun, Tasmania is, after all, more than ten times the size of our Lawns-tun, so we're well outnumbered. Let's not make too many assumptions here. I reckon that thinking outside the box occasionally may even be a good thing. The missus and I, for example, have realised that we rather like our friend's pronunciation of Ma-RAZ-eeyun. It rolls off the tongue better than the correct version, if you ask me, and we've started to say it like that deliberately in our house. At first it was for a laugh. But then it stuck, and it's only a matter of time until a Cornish person hears us saying Ma-RAZ-eeyun, and, quite possibly, judges us. And you know what? I don't care.

Fishing trip

2014

E very summer throughout my childhood, on a certain Sunday, my dad would charter a fishing boat from Newquay harbour (he'd partly grown up in Newquay and loved the place, always going misty-eyed whenever *'down 'arbour'* was mentioned. In fact twenty years ago we scattered his ashes off Newquay's harbour wall).

Father always booked skipper Reg Trebilcock and his little boat, Winnie, for our half-day's deep sea fishing. We'd catch pollack, gurnard, dogfish, bream, conger, all sorts. Our freezer-filling family fishing trip was a highlight of every summer in the late sixties and early seventies.

In the past few years I'd found myself thinking a lot about those childhood memories. So last summer I assembled nine friends (of widely differing angling ability) and chartered a boat myself. It was a thinly disguised, self-indulgent nostalgia trip as far as I was concerned. When I booked the trip in the spring, I'd had visions of grey, choppy seas, difficult decisions about when to cut our losses and turn back, seasickness and general woe. The usual 'glass is half empty' kind of stuff you've come to expect from your humble columnist, having been battered into submission by a life of disappointment and a succession of truly dreadful summers.

But no, this was July 2013, and the weather was perfect. Literally, perfect. It was to be the most incredible day. Within fifteen minutes of leaving harbour we were among dolphins. Loads of them. I'm no stranger to dolphins. I've seen them in Cornwall most years, and plenty further afield. But this! This was completely unexpected, intimate, spontaneous. They were so close to the boat we could practically reach out and touch them. And they stayed with us, sometimes at a distance, sometimes close up, on and off, all day.

Skipper Reg is long gone, but our skipper today (rather pleasingly) was his nephew, Dave, who was everything you'd expect from a Cornish boat skipper – all laconic charm and understated expertise, brown as a nut and dressed in nothing more than a pair of shorts, all day long (personally I'd have at least put a pair of flip-flops on, bearing in mind the incompetence of at least half the crew, and the rate at which fish hooks were flying about the place).

Dave took us miles to find just the right spot (it was an hour and a half before we even put a hook in the water). And when he finally cut the engine we found ourselves in another world – so far out we could barely see land, yet on such a still day that the surface of the water, even way out here, was like glass. The only sound was the tiniest of ripples gently kissing the hull of the boat, which was barely moving at all. It was looking increasingly unlikely that anyone would be seasick today. The sky, a deep, constant blue, had the thinnest layer of white cumulous, helpfully keeping the fiercest of the rays off. It was hot, but not burning.

Oh, and the fishing. Within a minute we landed our first good-sized pollack. This continued for hours, until we fancied a change. Adjusting our tactics we had ling, red and grey gurnard, mackerel and, er, a flatfish, as I recall. By the end of the trip an otherworldly atmosphere had pervaded our motley crew: one of quiet disbelief. We were reduced to an almost debilitating state of chilled-out contentment. This had been the most surreal of experiences. Our timing had been impeccable: a day-long fishing trip right in the middle of the loveliest summer we've had for years. Chugging into the harbour, we had so much pollack that we could barely carry our haul up the steps. Back at my place we barbecued some of it (high point: ling, low point: definitely pollack. It may be sustainable, but it's no cod). We sat in the garden in shirt sleeves til the early hours. A day you didn't want to end. A day to cherish.

And now I find myself questioning if that perfect day really happened. More importantly, I wonder whether I should organise a repeat trip this summer. All the chaps want to do it again. But how could we ever equal that?

Living the dream

2014

I 've had lots of comments from people about the introduction to my book, in which I decry the genre of books involving people with names like *Minty Fumble* leaving the big city to downsize and live the dream somewhere unfamiliar.

The protagonist in these books invariably starts out as a high flyer. Peter Mayle, whose *A Year in Provence* was so ubiquitous in the late eighties, had been creative director of a big advertising agency. King of the Cornish downsizers, Derek Tangye, produced a relentless barrage of bucolic tales for decades (you must remember *A Chaffinch in the Chimney*? *A Mole on the Mantelpiece*?). Where did he start out? Only MI5! Most recently, Tessa Hainsworth has brought us a series of books describing downsizing from London to work as a postie on the Roseland. Sure enough, the author was something senior at the *Body Shop* before downsizing to little old Cornwall.

Now, it obviously helps the storyline if the hero is intentionally rejecting a career and lifestyle others may covet. They've got more to lose. But isn't it all a bit obvious? There must be plenty of others downsizing to live the rural dream with fascinating stories to tell, but they'll never seduce the prospective publisher into reading beyond the first sentence without some superannuated lifestyle to kiss goodbye to.

Personally I've never been all that interested in reading about people downsizing. And yet I seem to have read quite a few. I read Peter Mayle in the eighties because everyone did. Just as we all bought that album by the Gipsy Kings. Likewise I remember *everyone* reading Derek Tangye in the seventies. Yet the subtext of such books always made me uncomfortable: that life in *'the country'* is, almost by definition, less complicated for everyone concerned. It isn't. Not in Cornwall anyway. Life here is hard. Not everyone's making a living making picture frames out of driftwood or painting pebbles off the beach. I look around me and I'm surrounded by people who are just as stressed as people in London. For doing a similar job, many are earning less than half the money. Cornwall is extremely expensive, there is appalling deprivation, and it's not getting any easier.

But I've been thinking about it, and I've had a bit of an epiphany. Maybe I've been overanalysing things. Tessa Hainsworth has identified a fundamental truth. No matter how stressed and miserable you are, in Cornwall you are never far from beauty. For most people, it really *does* represent a significant increase in the quality of life. We have no big cities. Popping down to a beautiful beach after work is a bit of a cliché, but whenever I do it, I think back to when I was a straphanging London commuter, surrounded by other commuters blankly staring, loathing it all, preying that some loony doesn't come and sit next to you, or a drunk doesn't throw up on your shoes. And that, truly, is a gift that keeps on giving.

So I've been thinking of writing a 'living the dream' book myself, as it does appear to be quite lucrative. Let me elaborate on the brief synopsis I touched on in the introduction to my book. Let's see now: Daily London commute and commitment to sustaining a vast salary become unbearably stressful...a catalyst event occurs, necessitating life-changing decision to relocate and chase a pastoral idyll...at least one family member is extremely reluctant...fundamentally flawed and virtually derelict Cornish business is acquired (lavender farm on a flood plain...organic cider-making business during succession of barren apple harvests...), kids are enrolled in quaint village school where there are only nine pupils and they still use a slate and a piece of chalk...a menagerie of interesting animals is acquired, including at least one improbably disabled dog or cat...old friends occasionally come to stay from London to highlight the change in lifestyle and create numerous comic scenes as he/she interacts with barely-intelligible locals...finally a flood/other natural disaster occurs, leading to landmark decision whether to throw in the towel or not. Conclusion: although it's all very difficult, it's better than commuting in London.

Sounds pretty viable doesn't it? All I need is a title.

Shed

2015

T hese days, you'd be hard pressed to think of a more ambiguous word than *shed*. When someone says 'I've been in my shed' you have no idea what they mean unless you've seen the shed in question. It's as meaningless as saying 'I work for the Council' or 'I'm Cornish'. They may have been rummaging among cobwebby boxes of Flymo bits and crusty paint tins in one of those cheapo, 6 x 4 foot flimsy shiplap jobs. But equally they may have been finalising a multi million pound deal in a bespoke studio full of well-paid employees from where they're running a global software empire.

Both are often considered 'sheds'. But more often than not, a shed is not a shed. At least, not in my dictionary's definition of 'a small building or lean-to of light construction, used for storage, shelter etc'. I'm surrounded by people working from, well, let's just call it 'a wooden structure in the garden'. If it's anything vaguely artistic, the buzzword is apparently no longer 'shed'; it's '*shedio*'.

Yet we delight in still referring to our outside structures as 'sheds', no matter how un-shedlike they may be. There's something quintessentially British about the inverted snobbery of it, a bit like calling your supermodel wife 'the missus' or a big splurge at *Nathan Outlaw* 'a fish supper'.

But it's not just that. When we talk about doing something *in the shed* it introduces a certain frisson – there's something a bit clandestine about going into your shed to get up to who-knows-what. I'm guilty of it myself. The anthology of this column is called '*Notes from a Cornish Shed*', because it sounds intriguing. The shed in question used to be a shed, but if I'm honest, it's definitely more of a, well, *garden office* these days. OK, *shedio* even. But that's the thing: I still call it a shed. Everyone does.

And I'm in good company. Some very impressive sheddy activity springs easily to mind. Roald Dahl famously was at his most creative writing by hand, sitting in an armchair, *in his shed*. In my house Dahl is the most popular author of all time (I'd vote for William Boyd, my wife would probably go with Barbara Kingsolver, but we're outnumbered by our twins for whom it's RD all the way – *Danny Champion of the World* reigns supreme). There can be no better example of people modestly achieving incredible things in sheds. They can be beguiling and inspiring places.

And I'm sure that many of us have visited arguably the coolest one in Cornwall. Or if not the coolest, at least the one with the best view: Hawker's Hut, set vertiginously on the coast path near Morwenstow. The eccentric Parson Hawker made it from wreck, a century and a half ago, to retreat to, and, allegedly, get off his face on opium. It's an enchanting place. Oh, except that it's not a shed. It's a hut – the clue's in the name. Crikey, when does a shed become a *hut*? Back to the dictionary.

This strange relationship we Brits have with our sheds has been taken to a whole new level in the past decade, with the advent of the national *'Britain's Favourite Shed'* competition. All the shortlisted sheds this year were amazing achievements, but I have to say very few could be described as a shed. The ones with the most charm had retained a sense of their innate 'sheddiness', rather than been transformed to the point of becoming something entirely different. My favourite had to be the chap who'd taken a normal shed, bolted it to a load of pallets, attached an outboard engine and launched it in the river. I was won over when I saw that he'd christened it *'Maid of Dekkin'*. To be honest, the day he put it in the water was the day I'd have started describing it as a raft, but no, apparently it's still a shed.

Truly, it seems there's just no limit to how far we can stretch this word.

A Victorian holiday

2010

O h no. Not November again.
I don't know if I can bear the thought of another winter. True, we've had a bad run of late. News stories always compare any slightly nippy winter with the notorious winter of '62-63, but my memories of that one are a little hazy on account of the fact that I spent it in Truro, flat on my back in a comfy, fully chromed Silver Cross pram with little to worry about beyond where my next rusk was coming from. But Mother tells me it was bad.

I doubt there have ever been two successive vile, sub-zero, relentlessly cold winters like the two we've just had. And the problem is, we'd all convinced ourselves that this is some kind of subtropical paradise. Honestly, it's enough to make the Cornish gardener abandon his tender exotics and grow something dreadful and commonplace. Like roses.

But all is not lost. Because in the midst of last January's horrific weather, something rather wonderful happened. Admittedly many Cornish villages, including mine, didn't actually experience more than a couple of inches of snow, but what did fall froze, and stayed frozen for days. And this created a whole new world. A sort of Victorian holiday. Little transitory microcosms were created where people chatted in the street, and shared cars, and, dare I say it, *rather enjoyed it all*. I talked to more neighbours than in the previous five years put together. It was lovely. It was, well, just plain *old fashioned*.

The otherworldly feel was intensified by the bird life. My garden was full of redwings, in huge numbers. In fact for the first time, I could properly appreciate one of the commonest Cornish phrases you'll ever hear: 'Wish't as a winnerd.' For the winnerds (redwings) were arriving in force, and they were starting to look more than a little wish't as the poor birds, exhausted and starving after their journey from even colder countries to the north, attempted to refuel and recover. What a sad sight they were. More than a few Cornish cat owners must have wondered why Tiddles turned his nose up at his tinned supper. Then, the redwings were joined by that other exotic winter thrush, the much bigger and even prettier fieldfare. And there were blackcaps and bullfinches in quantities I'd never previously seen.

The media did their best to scupper it all and turn us against each other. The whole situation was of course our fault in the first place, with man-made climate chaos being the cause of it all. Then there was uproar if the council didn't grit the roads and pavements constantly. Local radio contributed by inviting a friendly compensation lawyer in to encourage people to take legal action if they'd fallen over or crashed their car. Nice.

But even amid this obligatory 21st century negativity, you couldn't help but notice the Victorian holiday feel. I took a stroll down to the village on a Sunday afternoon, and although it was tricky walking, this meant that any meeting with an oncoming person necessitated a detailed conversation. The monochrome view of the beach from the coast path stopped me in my tracks; there's something about a beach covered in snow. It just looks, sort of, somehow, *wrong*. Like something that should just never happen. The scene before me could have been a Victorian picture postcard, a hazily remembered world, these days only enjoyed in a weekly episode of *Lark Rise to Candleford*. But here it had been temporarily revived for us all. This was a world where cars were momentarily of no use, and so kids, and indeed their parents, rode sledges down any available incline, and people strolled with abandon down the middle of the road, stopping to chat at any available opportunity ('how are we going to get to work...when will it end...is it worse than last year...?").

I've no idea what the coming winter has in store for us. But if it's another cold one, let's just remember, it's not necessarily all bad.

Chicken

2013

I just read an article about how several types of animal we previously considered among the most stupid, are actually surprisingly intelligent.

Apparently it's a myth that goldfish have a three-second memory. Pigs can use mirrors, and chickens have better numeracy and spatial awareness skills than young children (they didn't say how young). A professor of animal welfare at Bristol University told *The Times* that '*the domesticated chicken is something of a phenomenon…Studies over the past 20 years have revealed their finely honed sensory capacities, their ability to think, draw inferences, apply logic and plan ahead*'.

Good grief. I really can't imagine the chickens in my garden ever 'planning ahead', even in the loosest sense of the word.

But I can't help thinking that the main reason we dismiss chickens as daft is that they're so, well, *funny*. The comedy value of a chicken is surely unrivalled among animals. Monkeys come close. And who among us can resist a meerkat? But chickens are in a league of their own. You get rubber ones, you get people dressed up in plump-bellied chicken suits… and who hasn't clucked and flapped their elbows from time to time to imitate fear, or laying an egg? It's a funny noise. The chicken is even the star of the world's most commonly told (although decidedly unfunny) joke. See, I don't even need to tell it, because you know it. How many other jokes can you think of like that? Chickens walk funny. They sound funny. So it's easy to dismiss them as ridiculous.

But I have to say, when you actually watch a free-ranging chicken for a while, your opinion soon changes. I'm not claiming they're up there with, say, chimpanzees (in which case they'd have featured in the space programme in the early sixties. Which is, granted, quite a stretch of the imagination). But chickens definitely have individual personalities. Compared with my geese, for example, their intelligence is off the scale.

To be honest I'm a little disappointed in the geese – they're basically flocking, mindless, grass-chomping machines. Whereas your chicken is independent, frantically busy, clean, opportunistic and delightfully chatty. They're adorable when roosting. They're lots of fun to send to sleep by tucking their head under a wing and rocking gently (if only the same technique worked with twin boys). They are endearingly difficult to catch, unless they want you to, in which case they squat down, quivering, presumably in the blindly optimistic hope that they might be about to enjoy a spontaneous visit from a cockerel (which we don't have. Should they ever be graced by a real one I have a feeling that our virginal hens would get quite a shock).

They are also a remarkably effective little predator. Yes, predator. Just watch the way their eyes lock onto an airborne insect, then they launch themselves three feet vertically to grab it with their scaly beak. It's quite a surprise when you see it for the first time. I certainly didn't expect that of a chicken. It's a bit like when you discover that the three biggest killers in Africa are all vegetarian (hippo, elephant, buffalo. OK that's obviously one of those variable statistics, depending on which report you read. I'm not counting mosquitoes).

Anyway. We all know how popular chickens are to keep these days. From ramshackle, muddy old coops in fields to trendy, pink, moulded-plastic, design-statement coops on urban balconies, everybody's doing it. If you don't have any yourself I bet you know plenty of people who do. In Cornwall I'm sure we're above the national average. And I'm sure that the reason we've all gone fowl-crazy has a lot to do with how fascinating they are to watch. There's a lot of truth in this report about chicken intelligence. If, like me, you'd dismissed the humble chicken as dim-witted and bird-brained, take a closer look. You may be surprised.

Festival

2017

P hew, it's March. Thank goodness.

The only thing that's kept me going all winter has been looking forward to all those lovely music festivals. The proliferation of festivals in the UK these days is incredible, with new ones being launched every year (despite their reputation for being notoriously unprofitable). In fact in the last ten years, the number of festivals taking place annually in the UK has apparently gone from under 500 to over a thousand. Although I'm a relative newcomer to it all, I'm a complete convert. Especially now that I've been to Port Eliot.

Port Eliot Festival is the one held all over the stunning house and grounds of the St Germans family, up near Saltash in late July. I held out for years. Its achingly upper middle class reputation put me off, as well as the fact that it wasn't exactly a music festival (more of a literary festival, if you had to label it – no big name bands here). Plus, more significantly, I was here in its previous incarnation, the Elephant Fayre. The old Elephant Fayre has achieved a sort of mystical cult status these days – it was a bizarre, anarchic animal spawned in 1981 by the owner and, by all accounts, party animal, Peregrine Eliot, 10th Earl of St Germans, in which spaced-out hippies rubbed shoulders with leather jacketed punks. I'll admit that my memories of it are hazy. I remember naked people wandering around, and I remember performance poets like Ivor Cutler and Heathcote Williams – characters who seemed omnipresent in the scrumpified, art college world in which I was immersed for the entire duration of the early eighties. I remember sleeping in my dad's shop van, and someone juggling with rats, and that The Cure headlined. I remember my weekend ticket costing £12. And I remember that it was absolutely brilliant.

So the Elephant Fayre made me a bit snobby about going to any sort of reborn 21st century posh version. Every year, my wife and I would deliberate about whether this new Port Eliot incarnation was likely to be as good as people claimed. Our judgment was clouded by visions of champagne-quaffing *Guardian* readers down from Chelsea in their organic hemp yurts scoffing quinoa and kumquat porridge. But then we heard about the sad loss of Peregrine Eliot, the driving force behind the whole thing. Realizing that its days might be numbered, we decided it was time to pull our finger out and give Port Eliot a go. We'd take this kids. Bite the bullet. Embrace the quinoa.

The ticket price was a shock: £150 for one person and over £450 for a family. A considerable hike from the £12 I paid in 1983! But it was worth every penny – Port Eliot Festival was an otherworldly, exquisite microcosm with so many experiences on offer that it blew any preconceived reservations out of the water. There may have been people partaking of quinoa, but I simply looked the other way. My only regret was that you miss out on things because there's so much going on.

49

But enough of Port Eliot – there are so many festivals in the south west, varying enormously, and catering for all tastes. Thinking about it, I can recall quite a range I've been to over the past couple of years (and these are just the 'music' festivals): Looe Festival is spread all over the town, and deliciously timed in early autumn to squeeze the last dregs out of the summer. Dartmoor's Chagstock is as cosy and family-friendly as you could imagine. Perranporth's Tunes in the Dunes is more of a series of gigs in a cordoned-off area of the beach, which you leave at the end of the night, and return to the next day. At Tropical Pressure in Porthtowan (my local one), you have the most gobsmacking Atlantic view as backdrop to a smorgasbord of World Music.

All different in their own right, all with something distinctive to offer. But the most striking thing they all have in common (apart from all making me want to return the following year) is that none of them existed ten years ago.

A Cornishperson's duty

2008

I t's a good couple of years since I've even mentioned the word *chough* in this column. This is quite an achievement, considering my choughy book's been out almost a year (the critically acclaimed *Shadows in the Sky*, £6.99, available in paperback from all good....oh all right, this isn't really the place...). So I reckon any risk of 'But you just drone on about ruddy choughs all the time' accusations must be running at an all time low. So here goes.

That amazing, pioneering pair of choughs down on the Lizard have just completed an incredible seventh breeding season, producing four much-needed females to even up the current rather *blokey* population. For the third year running there's also been a second nest further up the coast. I make that a whopping 38 young choughs successfully fledged in Cornwall since their return here in 2001. Obviously nature being what it is, quite a few have disappeared or perished over the years, but the fact remains that we have a population of these gorgeous birds. A generation of kids are growing up in Cornwall barely aware that they went away. To them the chough isn't just some sad, lost legend – it's part of the scenery.

And yet, incredibly, there are Cornish people (proper Cornish, some of 'em), who still haven't made the pilgrimage down to the Lizard to try and spot a chough. To me that's behaviour about as Cornish as running out of turnip and settling for a bit of diced carrot when you're making a pasty. Or driving home over the Tamar bridge without screaming 'Oggy Oggy Oggy' at the top of your voice. You don't? Well, you should. I'd almost go as far as saying that it's a Cornishperson's duty to set eyes on a Cornish chough at least once before they die. They should learn 'em it in schools.

Now I have heard some people say, "But I'm not interested in birds". Well, that's not really the point. You don't have to be! Regardless of whether you're prone to twitching tendencies yourself, having choughs flying around Cornwall is still big news. They're our national bird. They're beautiful. They were extinct here. They're completely wild, not captive-bred birds that have been released. You no longer have to go to a zoo or to another country to see them. This is great. Really, really great.

I'll admit that other exciting things might be happening in Cornwall. Truro City may be winning at football. And we may be hosting the 2010 World Lifesaving Championships. They may be talking about doing a bit of mining again. And yes, there may be a great big greenhouse where once we had a great big china clay industry. *But the choughs are back. This is amazing!*

Why hasn't the Lizard become Cornwall's most visited tourist destination as thousands flock down there to catch sight of this charismatic, peerless, definitive symbol of Cornwall? It is, after all, way more significant than that black flag with the white cross of dubious origin named after a saint who was probably Irish (and now chiefly utilised by visitors as car stickers to proclaim 'I've been to Cornwall' the same as they might say 'I've seen the lions of Longleat'). And yes, more definitive than the much-abused pasty (not that I mind a pasty. With turnip, obviously). Choughs. In Cornwall. Real ones. I still can't quite believe it, seven years on. Why aren't we shouting it from the rooftops?

It's not as if it's that hard to find them, at least not in the spring. For seven years running, the original pair of birds, defying all the odds, have raised youngsters in the same cave, down at Southerly Point. That's dedication for you. Not only that, but true to our 21st century standards of wanting-everything-handed-to-us-on-a-plate, the nesting pair chose a site perfectly located for the lazy observer. Yes, they built their nest in a cave that's just across the bay from a friendly café. So during May and June you can sit there, stuffing yourself with delicious crab sandwiches and cream teas, and wait for the birds to fly in and out of the cave. Anyone who's spent time looking for rare birds will tell you that it doesn't get much easier than that. There's even been an RSPB guide standing there with a telescope, keeping watch on our behalf. Could they have made it any simpler to see this incredibly rare and precious bird?

Now that the 2008 chicks have fledged, the birds are spending a lot more time away from their cave, exploring the landscape, making a chough rather more of a challenge to find.

But what better excuse for a walk on the coast path, immersed in that stunning landscape? Or, assuming they nest at Southerly Point again next year, let's make a mental note to get down to the Lizard in 2009, to pay homage to our sacred bird. After all, a precious gift has been returned to us. Our dodo isn't dead after all. Come on. You owe it to yourself.

Kilt

2014

I 've just had an invitation to a wedding. It's in Cornwall, and I've got this overwhelming desire to wear a kilt.

I think a combination of factors have led to this. You certainly see a lot of tartan about these days, and a quick Google search tells me that sure enough, it 'will be one of the key autumn/winter 2015 trends in menswear'. Tartan, it seems, is super hip. Not just tartan though. Actual kilts. At *Lidl*, that novelty shopping experience where you go in looking for some basic groceries, and come out with an approximation of those groceries, but all spelled funny, plus a set of rechargeable screwdrivers and a cat gymnasium, you can now get, yes, *a kilt*. Or at least you could, leading up to Burns Night in late January. I'm not sure if they still stock them – I presume it depends on demand, but at £30 a pop I've got a feeling they might be onto something.

Pretty much every Cornish wedding I've ever been to has featured at least one guest in a kilt. If other chaps feel the way I do, then combined with the rising popularity of tartan, kilt wearing in Cornwall must be on the increase. I've been to a couple of weddings where all the ushers wore them, and they looked absolutely brilliant. After all, what says 'I'm a Cornishman, and proud of it!' better than strutting about dressed like a Scotsman in a tartan that hadn't even been invented when I was born?

OK, I'm being a little harsh – there's considerable evidence that although the Cornish national tartan was only created in 1963, plain kilts, usually black, were worn by Cornishmen going right back to the turn of the 20th century. The kilt may not be as integral to our world as it is to a Scotsman's, but it's common to Celtic nations, and we'm certainly o' they.

Anyway all that really matters to me is that Cornish kilts look really cool (although not literally – apparently they're sweltering). No matter if it's the Falmouth Marine Band, or the old boy down the pub, or an usher at a wedding, they always draw admiring glances. As far as the actual tartan's concerned, the ubiquitous saffron-coloured one, though still a novelty when I was a boy, is everywhere these days. It's immediately recognizable. The even nicer Cornish Hunting tartan is a tempting alternative, and a number of other versions now exist.

But as for actually wearing a kilt, I'm nervous. There's a lot to think about. All the paraphernalia for a start. The kilt bit is just the beginning - there's all the other stuff. I'd need a sporran of course, but I can't help thinking the full Prince Charlie jacket/white shirt/waistcoat/matching tie/brogues combo might just push me from a feeling of slight self-consciousness deep into a chasm of downright embarrassment.

Then there's the price: over a hundred quid to hire it all for the weekend, or several hundred if you want to buy just the kilt. I don't begrudge the price – it's a lot of gear. Eight yards of heavyweight woollen tartan goes into a proper kilt. But it's quite a financial hit for the wearer. Making that kind of purchase would mean a long term, proper commitment. I guess a Scotsman knows that he's probably going to dig his kilt out once a year for Burns Night, plus any weddings or funerals in between. But a Cornishman?

Above all, what about the actual reality of putting on a kilt? It's got to feel odd, at least at first. It's just so different to what a chap's used to wrapping around his legs. Outside his usual comfort zone, you could say. But I should be OK with that - the last time I wore a skirt it was 1982 and I was going through quite an interesting period at art college which, though just a phase, I rather enjoyed. Perhaps a bit too much.

Looks like I've got some thinking to do. I'll let you know what happens.

House guests

2003

T he hordes that descend at Easter, build up through May and June, then burst through the floodgates at the end of July are all part of life in Cornwall. 'Twas ever thus. Summer visitors are our lifeblood, and I can't remember a time when they weren't. As many of our old industries dwindle, we increasingly depend on tourism. It comes with the territory, and it is a good thing.

But there is one side effect of this phenomenon I have a problem with. It's a problem we natives all suffer from, yet dare not speak its name, lest someone should overhear and think they are not welcome. But I'm going to come right out with it: people inviting themselves to stay can be, well, *a bit much*. There, that's the blue touchpaper lit.

I should have realised something was going on as soon we moved back to Cornwall three years ago. That first summer, we had forty-two different people come to stay. That's right, *forty-two*. Some of them more than once. We weren't running a hotel, and we don't have an unusually large number of friends. Someone we know with similar contacts moved to the Midlands at around the same time, and in the same year, had four visitors. I'm saying nothing. OK, not true – I am saying something. I can't help it. The fact is, a week's holiday in some friends' cottage near the sea in Cornwall in August represents a considerable saving on the going rate. A one hundred per cent saving, you could say. But it doesn't do anyone any good, thinking like that.

It was partly our own fault. On our moving card we deliberately proclaimed: 'You are all welcome to come and stay!' What were we thinking? As it turned out we did lose touch with a handful of people who perhaps didn't think much of Cornwall, based on, perhaps, some mizzly childhood memory of a ruined chalet holiday in Trepiddle. But for most people, we suddenly became a whole lot more popular. From what I've heard, this is a familiar story.

Now don't get me wrong; generally it's nice having visitors. But you do have to know a few basic rules if you're going to keep your Cornish lifestyle as idyllic as it's supposed to be. And since there is no rulebook, you have to learn as you go along. In my house we've been compiling a sort of unofficial rulebook for the last three years, and we reckon we're getting pretty good at coping with the onslaught. Allow me to share with you a few basic principles:

1) *Don't overdo it.* Make sure your guests understand the house rules from the start. Upon arrival, they're acquainted with the essentials in the kitchen, shown to their room and given a front door key amid strong hints that they are expected to fend for themselves. That's if my wife's doing it. If it's me, they get something more along the lines of, "Your room's up there, the kettle's over there and the fridge is here. I expect you to replace what you consume. Now go to the beach". Never cook for your

guests, unless it is a very special occasion. Not even breakfast. You may throw them a few scraps from the table, if they look hungry. The worst thing you can do is cook a nice welcome dinner when they arrive, unless you make it blindingly obvious that this is simply a welcome gesture, on no account to be repeated. If you do fall into this trap, a dark atmosphere will descend on the house in the ensuing days of their stay as your expectant guests slowly realise that the 'welcome' meal was a one-off, and that you couldn't possibly sustain that level of hospitality. They'll wonder if it's something they said. This might seem a little harsh, but we like to think it's firm but fair. Cruel to be kind. It's worked for us.

2) *Save things up.* We all have our favourite places to visit, whether it's a beach, a particular walk, a trip to the Minack, whatever. But I'm convinced that many locals never visit these favourite places by themselves. And it's for good reason. What's the point in going there when chances are that within a few weeks someone will be staying who is desperate to go there? In this respect it can be nice to have house guests, and it forces us all to get out and do things.

It's the same as people living in London who say they only ever go to an art gallery or the theatre when they're showing foreign relatives around. The only down side is that on the rare occasion when you don't have summer guests, you just hole up and wait for the next deluge. It's becoming rare for us to even take a walk to the cliffs, less than ten minutes away, because we've become conditioned to associating such activity with other people.

However, even though you are going to one of your favourite places, remember that your guest may have very different expectations to you. I've lost count of the number of times a winter visitor has proclaimed 'I love Cornwall in the winter – that's when it's at its best! There's nothing nicer than a bracing walk across a windswept beach in February!' So you take them to Godrevy at low tide, having supplied them with sufficient gear because they left theirs at home because they thought it would be warmer, and after two minutes on the beach, they're saying 'It's freezing! What about going for a hot chocolate?' You have to learn to predict situations like this. If you are at all suspicious that things could get ugly, err on the side of caution. Don't go. You'll only upset yourself.

3) *Manipulate shamelessly.* Certain places are very popular, so unless you want to visit Eden once a fortnight for the rest of your life, adopt the principle that you only go somewhere if you feel like it. A truly manipulative host will drop subtle hints, in order to subliminally steer the guest in the direction of a place he himself would actually like to go. 'I've heard the early evening light on Brown Willy is quite beautiful this time of year.' That type of thing. I tried this one summer's day last year when we had an Australian visitor staying, and it worked beautifully. Despite its titillating title, we all felt that a stroll up to the highest natural point in Cornwall would be a good idea. And we were right. As we rose from the miasmal mists of Bodmin Moor and made the gruelling ascent of the north face of that majestic peak we were glad we'd made the effort. Especially as we reached the summit and a curious expression

61

came over our antipodean friend's face as she sighed and exclaimed, 'Gosh. This certainly puts Ayers Rock into perspective'. I was so proud. 'Wait til you see Carn Brea,' I said.

4) *Empower*. Put a big map of Cornwall up on the wall somewhere prominent. Ideally pin it to the ceiling above their bed and rig the bedside light so they can't turn it off. They'll be thinking for themselves in no time. I thought of this when I realised how much time we were wasting poking at a crumpled map of Cornwall suggesting activities every time we had new arrivals.

5) *Aversion*. To a certain extent you can avoid the blight that is an unwanted house guest in the first place. Simply be economical with the truth. I'm the worst liar in the world, but on the telephone, no-one can tell that you're avoiding eye contact, so I can get away with saying 'Actually, someone's already coming that week' when you get that all-too-familiar phone call. On one occasion a couple who hadn't been in touch for three years, despite all our cards, phoned and gaily left the following message: 'We're going to be in Cornwall at the weekend and wondered if we could crash at yours for a few nights. With the kids'. In August. When we were already double booked. We panicked. Sadly lacking the nerve to phone them back, we resorted to the very British 'bury your head in the sand to avoid a potentially embarrassing confrontation' tactic. We didn't answer the phone for a fortnight for fear they might call again.

So this August bank holiday, as last week's guests finally finish their leisurely breakfast and say their goodbyes, and you know you've only got an hour 'til the next lot appear in the drive, and then someone phones to say 'We were just in the area and thought we'd pop in with the new baby as we're driving back to London after lunch,' and you feverishly strip the beds, hoover, and go to the shops, but resist the urge to buy a nice piece of fish for a welcome dinner, just remember, if we all just observe a few simple rules, we can get through this thing.

Living in Cornwall is idyllic. It says so in all the magazines.

Mussels

2011

I had another perfect moment recently.

It was a stunning day; one of those slightly-above-freezing, still, winter days, not a cloud in the sky, the sun in your face, low over the horizon, making you blink, and grin, and dare to hope that spring might be just around the corner. I found myself with half an hour to spare before picking my up boys from preschool, which happens to be right by the beach. Coincidentally, the tide was as low as I've ever seen it. So I went for a quick stroll.

Deliberately inhaling lungfuls of sharp, life-affirming air, I headed, in my wellies, to the most distant rocks, left high and dry by that low, low tide. And on the rocks, there they were. It's been years since I've picked mussels from the beach, but I always have to have a look when there's a low tide. And I just couldn't resist these beauties. I didn't even have a bag on me, so, not wanting to muck up my jacket pocket, I picked a big handful, then headed back up the beach. We got home, and in no time I'd given the mussels a quick scrub, yanked out their little beardy bits, and fried them up in a bit of butter and garlic. A perfect moment: stunning day, beach walk, fabulous fresh mussels for lunch, all quite unexpected. Cornwall. What a place.

A few weeks before, I'd watched some of Channel 4's *Big Fish Fight* week, in which celeb chefs revealed various piscatorial atrocities in the hope of putting things right. Most significant was the unfathomable discarding of over-quota fish species. The waste of fish was sickening. We viewers learned other unsavory truths: the plight of factory-farmed salmon and their feeding habits, and that the wording on so-called 'dolphin-friendly' tins of tuna can be very misleading indeed. I happily signed Hugh Fearnley-Whittingstall's online petition.

I chatted to an eco-savvy friend about it, and asked him if he'd signed the petition too. "Nah," he replied, "It's all a bit obvious, really, isn't it? I mean, in Cornwall we do all that stuff anyway. We've all known for years that we should avoid buying cod in the chip shop, and factory-farmed salmon is bad, and all that stuff".

I suppose he was right, sort of. I'm pretty confident most of us in Cornwall are aware of the issues in the *Big Fish Fight*, at some level. But my friend was wrong to assume that we all act on this awareness in any significant, positive way. Just because we live here doesn't mean we all live our lives with an exemplary environmental conscience, sea-wise. Cornish supermarket shelves are piled just as high with cheapo factory-farmed salmon and indiscriminately harvested tuna, as anywhere else.

Just because we are surrounded by fish doesn't mean we have a particular affinity with their plight. My grandmother, who spent 101 years of her life in rural Cornwall, didn't even like fish, always greeting prawns like a fussy teenager: "Yuk!

Like eating little maggots!" I can clearly remember her saying.

I've always considered myself environmentally aware, and I've always loved fish, but I have to admit I've lost touch lately. There's a wet fish shop two miles from where I live, but I'm always forgetting to pop in. Mackerel is sustainable, cheap, and as tasty as almost anything from the sea. There are places you can buy three for a pound in the summer. But I can't remember when I last ate a fresh mackerel. The *Big Fish Fight* told us that mussels are about the most sustainable seafood we have in this country. "Go on, get out and buy some now!" urged Jamie Oliver, infectiously enthusiastic as ever. I don't even have to buy them. There they are, minutes walk from my house, fully available, fresh, for nothing. As long as there's an 'r' in the month, of course.

That's it then. I'm going to get back in the fishy zone. That half hour on the beach was more than just a perfect moment. It was a wake-up call.

Time zone

2016

S o, November. To be honest, it's probably no-one's favourite month. Unless it's your birthday I suppose. But as we get used to the clocks going back and the onset of those interminably dark winter evenings, I'm reminded of a conversation I had on a train this summer.

Returning to Cornwall from London, I'd got chatting to the lady sitting next to me. It was late afternoon on a Friday, the weather forecast looked good, and the weekend was full of promise. The lady was coming down straight from work to join her husband and kids for the weekend at the Bedruthan Hotel. But she was becoming a little concerned about the logistics of alighting at Bodmin Parkway, and then finding a taxi to get her to her Newquay destination before it got dark.

"Don't worry," I calmly reassured her, trying to be all 'I'm Cornish and I know about these things'. "You'll be sipping sundowners on your balcony well before dark".

She looked at me doubtfully, which I took to be an invitation to step it up a notch: "Don't forget – it gets dark twenty-two minutes later in Cornwall!" My travel companion's doubtfulness now turned to downright incredulity, which, to be honest, remained in her eyes until she disembarked at Bodmin Parkway.

I must have been trotting out this bit of trivia to people, especially holidaymakers, for at least thirty years. I probably read it somewhere once. But having now done some actual research for the purposes of this article, I see that 'twenty-two minutes' is slightly inaccurate. The time difference obviously varies throughout the year: the sun actually sets in Penzance twenty-five minutes later than in London at this time of year. In May, it's seventeen minutes later. But I'm thinking twenty-two minutes is an acceptably user-friendly compromise. It's quite a decent amount of time – no wonder people notice the difference. That extra light must genuinely enhance many visitors' holiday experience; enough time to enjoy an extra pint in the pub beer garden, just one more game of footie on the beach, or of course, G&T on your sun terrace.

Twenty-two minutes is practically a time zone, if you consider those mini time zones, like they have in Newfoundland. And of course, a mere two hundred years ago, we did have time zones in this country. I suppose this made sense, when you think of the distance between, say, London and Bristol (which had a ten minute time difference). In the late eighteenth century it would have taken Ross Poldark ages to travel by coach from London to Truro – he'd have simply adjusted his pocket watch now and again along the way (ha! Just managed to sneak in a subtle little *Poldark* reference there).

But then as we neared the mid 1800s, everything changed with the rapid development of telegraphic communications and a national rail network. Imagine running a rail system with fractionally different time zones all over the country! It's all very well in a colossal country like Canada, where I once adjusted my watch five times on a single journey from east to west, but in a small country like ours, it was obviously a recipe for disaster. A new, standardised system was introduced, called 'Railway time'. The Great Western Railway played a big part – yet another thing for which to thank Isambard Kingdom Brunel.

These days, it's unthinkable that there might be somewhere in the UK where the time is not exactly the same as the one on our watch (OK, *phone*). Not only that, but we expect to know that time, accurate to within a second.

I'll never know if the lady on the train ever made it to her hotel in time for cocktail hour on the sun deck. But if she did, I just hope she took a moment to gaze at the sunset and think to herself 'Well well, maybe that bloke on the train wasn't quite such a twit after all'.

Shark

2006

Here it comes again. The holiday season. I wonder what we'll find to terrify us this year. Last summer, it was a spate of news stories about dangerous sharks in Cornish waters. First it was a mako shark at Godrevy. Then there were reports of bull sharks, and a blue shark, and then I lost count.

There's nothing like a 'dangerous animal on the loose' story to get us going, particularly as we live in a country where all the bears and wolves were driven to extinction hundreds of years ago. It brings out the caveman in us, reminding us of a time when we had real, primal fears of being attacked and eaten by a wild animal. I suppose we do have adders – a potentially lethal snake – but one that hasn't killed anyone in this country for over twenty years. Most people have never even seen an adder, let alone been savaged by one.

So what a juicy opportunity for a bit of mass hysteria when a tourist reckons they've spotted a killer shark. *'Mako spotted in Cornish waters'* certainly makes a better headline than *'Nervous holidaymaker mistakes driftwood for killer shark they once saw in a film'*.

Jaws, it must be said, is a brilliant suspense film. Apart from certain scenes featuring a rather unconvincing rubber shark, it appeals to all those basic fears, the most obvious that of being hunted by a predator you can't see, but you fear is there. The scene where all the macho big game fishermen are clamouring to go and catch the killer shark is a classic.

Now it may be true that some species of shark known to occasionally attack people have been spotted in British waters once or twice. But as far as I know, no-one has ever been attacked by one here. Not ever. This media hysteria does no-one any good at all. Panicky headlines about killer sharks induce a completely bogus state of anxiety among the public, at a time when many shark species are seriously endangered. It's been well documented that our basking sharks are having to head north to find enough plankton to eat. Whatever sharks remain in Cornish waters we should welcome, not fear.

So what went wrong last summer, I hear you cry, when Cornish lifeguards removed dozens of people from the water at Godrevy because someone thought they'd seen a mako? Why would they to do this if a) it was unlikely to actually be one, and b) it didn't mean any harm? Perhaps they were just playing it safe – you can imagine if the lifeguards had let everyone stay in the water, and someone had coincidentally stepped on a weaver fish. "You were told there was a killer mako in the water," the victim might have sobbed, "*And yet you did nothing! And now I've hurt myself!*" As if the poor lifeguards didn't already have enough to worry about, what with it having been their busiest recorded summer ever. Perhaps a big sign saying "*You are a million times more likely to be killed by ignoring the flags than by a killer shark!*" would help.

Not that I feel sorry for the lifeguards. OK they have an incredibly responsible job, requiring a level of fitness, training and levelheadedness that most stockbrokers on twenty times the salary would fall well short of. But they also get to spend a lot of time driving quad bikes and twin cab pickups, getting a tan, and looking generally enigmatic. Lifeguards are about as cool as it gets, there's no two ways about it. And as for their clothes, I'm not exactly sure when they suddenly started looking so much better, but I suspect Baywatch had something to do with it. In what can only be called a Hasselhovian fashion makeover, the little skull caps and speedos of the past have long since given way to a far more stylish world of red shorts, wraparound shades and luminous sunblock.

But I digress. I saw something sharky happen on my local beach last summer that gave me hope. The dorsal fin and tail of the biggest basking shark I've ever seen appeared a couple of hundred yards out. It was innocently cruising along, and heading directly towards several hundred bathers. It was exactly like a scene from *Jaws*. The lifeguards, cool as you like, announced on their loudspeaker that a perfectly harmless basking shark was heading towards them all, and instead of the hysterical fleeing of my imagination, people stopped and calmly watched the spectacle. The shark then slowly dipped below the surface and presumably went on its merry way. So it seems there's hope. We're not all believing the hype.

I must admit it would have been pretty interesting if one of the bathers had screamed and disappeared under the water though. You know, just for a laugh.

Peak exotica

2017

This time of year, I've noticed a lot of people go a bit crazy putting photographs of their garden on *Facebook*. To be honest, I'm still struggling with the whole *Facebook* thing, clinging as I do to the outdated notion that events still occur in one's life even if they are not incessantly documented upon one's wretched telephone.

That said, I've never felt a more overwhelming urge to join in and start snapping. In fact I'm going to, because my garden is looking utterly spectacular. But I mean that in the way that your house might look 'utterly spectacular' if you painted it dayglo pink, or bungeed a ten-foot inflatable effigy of Donald Trump to its roof. It's not necessarily 'utterly spectacular' in a good way. My garden, at the moment, is not so much a triumph of horticulture as one of, well, *vulgarity*.

Let me explain. Three years ago I did a friend a favour and removed some dead tree echiums from their garden. For anyone not familiar with this plant (or who hasn't heard me going on about them before), tree echiums are those colossal spikes of blue flowers you see in early summer, looking as if they'd be more at home in a Dr. Seuss book. They're beloved of butterflies and bees, and originate in the Canaries. They add a touch of the exotic to any sunny, sheltered spot, usually going from germination to expiration in two years. Being a biennial, each plant then produces a vast number of seeds, most of which won't make it to adulthood. The botanical equivalent of a frog and its tadpoles.

Anyway, I stripped all the seeds off one of these dead echiums and produced many hundreds of perky little echium seedlings. Again like the tadpoles, a young echium is vulnerable in a winter cold snap. But they do well in Cornwall due to our mild winters, and I've had success with them before (they're actually dead easy to grow in a bit of rubbishy soil). With all this available stock, I planned to step things up a notch. I wanted to go for the ultimate sub-tropical Cornish garden effect. I aimed to reach a state of *peak exotica*.

Oh yes, against my better judgment, I planted those little seedlings everywhere. There must have been a hundred or more of them. I then spent the winter of 2015-16 anxiously checking the long-range weather forecast with a roll of horticultural fleece constantly at the ready, just in case there was a sharp frost.

By spring last year I was breathing a sigh of relief. But then they just sat there, making no attempt whatsoever to shoot skywards and flower. I realised that my plants were perhaps leaning more towards the *tri*-ennial side of things than the bi-ennial, and I reluctantly accepted that I was going to have to wait another year. Sure enough, by March this year, the little darlings were emerging from their second winter and visibly champing at the bit to let rip and shoot for the stars. Which they then proceeded to do. In spectacular fashion.

I'm now standing here, gazing upon the gobsmacking fruition of my ambition: dozens and dozens of teetering blue towers, almost everywhere I look in the garden. It took three years, but my patience has paid off dramatically. Most of them are well over ten feet tall, and so laughably out of scale with everything else in the garden, that when I venture out there, it feels more like Lilliput than Tenerife.

I can't decide whether it's just plain vulgar or not. Perhaps I shouldn't be so hard on myself – I honestly think it looks pretty cool. This is what I wanted, after all, and it certainly does look exotic. The important thing I need to remember is to remove them pronto before they set seed, or I could be looking at a good hundred thousand of the monsters by 2020.

Now, I'd definitely have to put a photo of *that* on *Facebook*.

The *Poldark* effect

2015

I know it's been hard to avoid the mounting hype for the past year, but can it be, can it *really* be, that *Poldark* is back? I still can't quite believe this is really happening. It's been such a part of our lives for so many decades, the very thought of it being re-done still seems like some sort of surreal dream. I know it's real, yet I still can't quite get my head around it.

Until you stop to think about it, it's easy to underestimate just how much *Poldark*'s affected us in Cornwall. I've just counted two dozen *Poldark* books in my house in various editions, including six editions of *Demelza* alone (those belong to the missus, who seems to have accumulated *Demelzas* without even realising it). Until recently we had most of the old episodes on video, only discarding them when we realised that we no longer had a machine capable of playing them. True, in my house we might be a little more *Poldarky* than most – it's Winston Graham's fault in more ways than one, because he once told my wife that he was considering using her name for a character in his next book – she couldn't get to sleep for weeks.

Poldark books are tucked away like this in most Cornish homes, as predictable as the little stained glass lighthouses that hang by suckers from our patio doors, or last year's tide tables down the back of our kitchen radiators. I don't honestly remember how many of the books I've read, because it was so long ago, and they sort of merge with the seventies TV show. *Poldark*, in all its manifestations, is everywhere. When I come to think about it, we named one of our geese Clowance. We'd have called one of our boys Ross until we remembered that our surname is Cross. Most of us know someone called Demelza (or cat, in the case of my Cornish ex-pat Canadian uncle).

Poldark is synonymous with Cornwall. It's become a part of us. But I'm not going to waste your time here by telling you what I think of the new TV version (the series has only just started at the time of writing). We all have our allegiances. It's a bit like James Bond. A vast new audience is going to love it – a fast-paced, sexed-up, well-acted, 21st century take. It's riveting, this Aidan Turner/Daniel Craig rebirth. At the same time many, especially older viewers, may remain loyal to the original Sean Connery Bond/Robin Ellis *Poldark*. There may even be a tiny minority of pedants claiming that the one-off George Lazenby Bond (or even the very early David Niven incarnation) is best, like the doomed 1996 ITV *Poldark*. Of course, true afficionados know that in the background, authors Ian Fleming and Winston Graham hold the key to it all. Without their inspirational books, none of this would even be happening.

I see no reason to endlessly deliberate over how the new *Poldark* compares with the seventies series we hold so dear. This is not an adaptation of that seventies series – it is a 21st century adaptation of a series of wonderful books, for a whole new audience, and it's fascinating to see a fresh realisation of something so familiar. Like a very old friend showing up on our doorstep – barely recognisable, but at the same time more lovable than ever.

No matter where our allegiances lie, the most important legacy for both TV versions, almost four decades apart, will surely be their influence on visitor numbers. Many argue that the seventies series kickstarted a sort of *new age* of Cornish tourism. If thousands of 'telly tourists' visit Port Isaac because they've watched *Doc Martin*, imagine how they're going to flock to the Lizard, and West Penwith, and Charlestown. Aidan Turner is pretty easy on the eye, but the Cornish landscape is even easier.

So brace yourselves Cornwall – it's going to be quite a ride.

Capital of Culture?

2017

C rikey. I don't think the phone lines on the *Radio Cornwall* lunchtime show have been this busy since the infamous 'One Cornwall' logo debacle of '09.

At the time of writing, councillors have just voted to support a bid for Truro to become the 2023 'European Capital of Culture'. The phones practically went into meltdown as irate members of the public jostled to chuck in their two penneth. I swear I could actually hear the steam coming out of their ears. Half a million quid was the figure being quoted to push Truro's bid to the next level, competing with the likes of Leeds, Dundee and Milton Keynes. And that's just for starters. If the bid gets through to the next stage then the actual figure required is, we're told, likely to run into many millions.

Now, we're living in a time of austerity and economic uncertainty that is unprecedented for many of us. It goes without saying that that kind of money would help a lot of public services to limp along through such hard times: libraries, public toilets, busses. Not to mention social care. No wonder people are mad. The sensible-sounding mayor of Bristol reluctantly announced that they were pulling the plug on their city's bid to become European Capital of Culture: "... there's no guarantee we'd win it...at a time when we're facing horrific budget decisions – it wouldn't be a wise way to spend the money".

And yet it seems plucky old Cornwall Council is still going to go for it. When it comes to the Council, people tend to be very suspicious. An above-the-national-average 56% of Cornwall voted to leave the EU last year, despite all the funding that's come our way. Now we'll be asking them to hand us a prestigious award, even though we will no longer be members.

Maybe that's delusional. I'm in no doubt that if the bid was successful, it would be a fantastic thing for Cornwall, creating huge media attention, and a much-needed boost to our economy. In 2008, when Liverpool held the exalted position, the city apparently enjoyed an economic impact of £800 million. In less lean and hungry times, I might well be saying "Hell yes – speculate to accumulate! Let's give it a go!" But I can't even remember when I last felt that positive about anything.

As I mentioned only last month, Truro's come a long way since the dreary place I remember from my childhood in the sixties – we've got the City of Lights parade, Gay Pride, and we might even see a proper sports/concert stadium built here within our lifetime. Nevertheless it still isn't exactly blessed with the panoply of cultural and artistic events that other far larger cities upcountry enjoy. But here's the thing: 'Capital of Culture' doesn't just refer to the city itself, but the whole county, of which it is the capital. And who can argue that Cornwall doesn't have an impressive artistic and cultural scene, both historically and in the present day? Mind you I've never been to Milton Keynes. Actually I did once. It was mostly roundabouts, as I recall.

I remember five years ago, how uneasy many of us felt before the first day of the Olympic Torch Relay that began at Lands End. I sceptically thought it would be a bit of a damp squib. But from dawn til dusk, it turned out to be the most surprising, memorable, emotional experience. Immaculately planned and executed, the whole spectacle looked stunning on people's televisions all over the world. Cornwall did it, with knobs on. What a feeling it gave us. How lovely if we could get that feeling back.

I've no idea whether we've got any chance of winning this bid. We could be sitting here in six years' time cursing the Council for wasting millions on a vanity project, or we could be proudly enjoying the fruits of our new status as European City of Culture. Either way, after Brexit and the election of the current American president, I'm willing to believe that absolutely anything can happen. Perhaps it will.

* *A few weeks later, the new leader of Cornwall Council predictably announced that Truro was withdrawing its bid. Go Milton Keynes!*

Keith

2003

W hen my wife and I returned from two years abroad and moved into our cottage on the north coast, it was all a little daunting. How would we take to the rural life? Who would our new friends be? Of course it all worked out fine. Everything slotted into place. But we did need to alter our expectations in certain areas. My best friend, as it turned out, was a little brown bird.

Very early on during the first year in our cottage, I became aware of an even-friendlier-than-most-robins robin, who I named Keith. In fact I claim to have met him before we even saw the house, when we came to look at the place for the first time. As we pulled up, anxious for my first view of the house and garden from the separate front drive, I peered through the hedge. And there he was, just a few feet away, on the big honeysuckle, as if to welcome us. At least that's what I like to think. He sensed how much I love birds and wanted to show me. "There's lots of us through here – come and see!" he seemed to be saying. It was a good omen.

Around the time we moved into the cottage, I visited a local second hand bookshop, and came upon a fantastic little paperback called *The Life of the Robin*, published in 1953, with a sweet little drawing of one on the front. The author, David

Lack, studied them for decades, including a four-year study of the robin population on a twenty-acre area in Devon, during which time he'd ringed a staggering 119 birds. What this book didn't tell me, I didn't need to know. About robins, obviously.

Thanks to Mr Lack, everything Keith did now had a perfectly rational explanation. I was aware that the little bird might actually have been a little lady robin – there is no discernible difference – and I read that it's an eighteenth century myth that the female is a slightly drabber version of the handsome male. Apparently people also used to believe that the wren was actually a female robin! I didn't care about such details. Keith was already a little geezer to me.

During that first year in the house, I spent a lot of time in my new office, which overlooked the front garden. Keith was very much in evidence from day one. It only took a few weeks of giving him little handouts to encourage him closer and closer, until he'd come straight to my outstretched hand for scraps. He was my little Robin Goodfellow, showing up when he felt like it, but making my day whenever he did. "You want to be giving him mealworms," said our knowledgeable neighbour, mindful that I didn't just stuff him with cake.

Of course I'm under no illusions that the real reason he was the friendliest bird in the garden right through the spring was that he was raising young, and appreciated the handouts. This was quite a thing to witness. He was killing himself trying to keep his young supplied. I never found the nest, and at first I never saw the little ones. Just excited little buzzing noises, deep within the shrubbery, seconds after he'd flown in there with some tit-bit. But then slowly, as their flying skills improved, they'd get braver, these little, fluffy, speckledy balls of feathers, looking more like tubby sparrows than any relative of my robin. And slowly they got bolder, and came out into the open more and more. There were four, although they were so quick that I wouldn't guarantee there weren't more.

But as the fledglings grew in confidence, so did the magpies. In the height of the late spring, every few minutes, a pied missile seemed to swoop in horizontally, terrifying whatever little bird it was vaguely aiming at. I never saw any magpie make contact, but one day, about a week after Keith's fledglings started appearing, they were nowhere to be seen. Almost overnight. I can only suspect the worst, as they certainly didn't look ready to be independent.

My little robin behaved strangely for a while. He definitely wasn't as friendly. But within a few weeks, buzzing noises were coming from the shrubbery again. And Keith was suddenly friendlier than ever. It was a second brood! I checked in *The Life of the Robin*. This was textbook stuff. Just like before, the little brown bundles with their stumpy wings started appearing, but five this time. And Keith was frantically busy. By now there seemed to be fewer magpies around, and most of this new brood made it, at least further than the first batch. I even started trying to name them, but it was impossible. They got slimmer, and less speckled, and then slowly, slowly, started to go a ruddy colour on their front. And then one by one they disappeared. All but one. And that one, after all that his dad had been through all summer, nearly did him in. Every day they scrapped. Keith would join me for lunch at the garden table, as he did every day, when his rival's piercing song would start. Keith would bristle, hop about a bit, then go and join his adversary, who by this time was looking more or less identical to his dad, for another confrontation.

But as time went by, they seemed to reached a compromise – some birdy treaty which gave Dad one side of the garden, and Junior the other. And it stayed pretty much like that. Fortunately the kitchen door and my office are on Keith's side, so I still saw quite a bit of him. But for various reasons we had to move the garden table to Junior's side of the garden. Dad never again joined me for lunch at the garden table. I dined alone. Son of Keith never became as friendly.

Keith and Junior only looked like each other for a week or two. Because just as Junior got prettier, during August Dad went into a terrible decline. Pale, thin, and nearly completely bald on his head, I was almost ashamed to introduce him to guests. I could hardly get a conversation out of him. I feared the worst. Only once had I been concerned for him before. I'd come out of the kitchen on a particularly warm summer's day, to find him sprawled on the path, wings spread and motionless. I thought he must have flown into a window, and slowly bent over to look closer. At the last moment, he flew away, and it turned out that he'd just been sunbathing. It became his little party piece for guests during the summer, that and his little dust baths.

Anyway Keith's decline was short-lived. By October his feathers had grown back, he'd put on weight, and he was redder than a Christmas card, which was very convenient, because I took some photos of him for our cards, looking very much his best. Chubby and relaxed, life was good for Keith. He seemed to have plenty of food to keep him going, despite the lean winter months. He'd done pretty well for himself. He'd made a lot of friends, and he didn't mind letting himself go a bit. Sort of like a little fluffy Elvis.

Perhaps he was entering his dotage, because I saw him less and less. The following spring I occasionally spotted him, but it could just as easily have been someone else. Three years is a good innings for a robin, the book says. The end of a lovely little era for me. And proof that you really don't need a red deer or a spoonbill in your garden to get excited about the wildlife. You just need to get close to it.

Touching the wild

2015

C orrect me if I'm wrong, but there aren't many people out there who quite enjoy a bit of camping now and again. It's too much of a Marmite type of activity. You either do a lot of it, or none at all. I bet as you read this you're either thinking 'Camping! Eugh! I can't think of anything worse!' or 'Ah, camping. I *love* it'.

For those of us who love it, sometimes it's hard to say exactly why. It certainly feels like an odd sort of paradox – when you're camping you're constantly busy, but at the same time, it's curiously relaxing. When you camp, you enter a parallel universe in which you're always doing little jobs, but you know deep down that none of them really matter. This summer a friend and I must have spent a good hour working out how to rig up a temporary clothesline. Cooking a meal takes a disproportionate amount of time and effort. But it doesn't matter – camping disengages you from real life and your troubles back home, while keeping your mind occupied with supposedly important daily activities. I'm telling you, it's useful therapy.

As for the Marmite issue, I think the key to unlocking the pleasure of camping for anyone is to find the level you're comfortable with. When you find it, and embrace it, you're a happy camper. There are infinite ways to go camping. In France this summer we watched a couple on a cycling tour pitch their comically weeny bivouac shelter across the path from a similar looking couple in a huge recreational vehicle complete with air con and a hundred TV channels. They didn't have much in common, but they did have one thing: they were both camping. They both wanted to have a natural outdoor experience. To touch the wild. But to very differing degrees. We all have to find our own level. I have a feeling that even those at the negative end of the Marmite scale simply haven't quite found their level yet.

My family and I found ourselves camping more than usual this year – in fact at the time of writing we're about to fit in one last trip before the clocks change and we all hibernate for six months. We've finally arrived at our perfect level you see. Grudgingly admitting that our leaky old tent was past it, we replaced it with a reliably waterproof one. What a difference. We were also shamed into replacing our ancient, wafer thin, foam sleeping mats by a family we met at a campsite on the Roseland who openly laughed at our sleeping arrangements. "I haven't seen those since I was in the army!" scoffed the dad, gazing at our old mats. And although I was inwardly mocking what I judged to be his own ludicrous level of luxury, I knew he was right. He sensibly recognised the need for a bit of comfort. My wife and I were clinging to a tortuous sleeping arrangement that had lingered on from our backpacking days. But nowadays I'm the wrong side of fifty, and I was waking up every morning feeling like I needed a hip replacement. So we bought a blow-up airbed, and we never looked back. In fact that airbed's more comfy than my mattress at home. It's changed everything.

The chosen level at which the missus and me did most of our serious camping many years ago, was very different. Back then, we carried those very same rolled-up sponge sleeping mats on our backs, together with a tiny dome tent. We duct taped that tent to the deck of Alaskan state ferries, and we splinted its cracked poles when they fell foul of Namibian sand storms. Camping like that literally unlocked a world of travel options. The squabbling devils kept us awake at night in Tasmania, as did the midnight sun in the Yukon. This summer it was a sunburned family from Birmingham who kept us awake. Fifteen miles from home, we were in a tent four times the size, and everything's changed. We've got airbeds and little boys, and a more expensive tent, and we camp because it gives us options right on our Cornish doorstep.

It's still camping, and it's still great.

Wet

2013

I wouldn't normally go on about the weather, but I do feel that something needs to be done. Summer approaches, and let's face it, it's probably going to happen again. You know what I'm talking about. We've had year after year of awful summers. And last year, well, it went way beyond the usual disappointing, unreliable anticlimax we thought we were getting used to.

Oh yes, summer 2012 really stepped it up a notch. Apart from a freak fortnight of sweltering sunshine in March, and a brief bit of respite in July, that was it. *'Worst summer in 100 years!'* the headlines proclaimed. It took bad summers to a whole new level.

It was biblically bad. So bad, in fact, that it was almost good, because it was so remarkable in its awfulness. It's provided us with a yardstick by which all future awful summers will be judged: the other end of the scale from the summer of '76. Just as we all recount that year when the lawns turned brown and hosepipes were banned and we Cornish spent hours on end in the sea without wetsuits and didn't get cold (it's true!), we'll describe summer 2012 as the year we had so much rain that lawns and flowerbeds grew at an unprecedented and terrifying rate.

I have never cut the grass as many times as I did last summer. I have never seen weeds grow like it. We gardeners just stood there, hands on hips, gazing at our herbaceous borders, thinking, 'I normally keep this bed in check with a bit of light hoeing; why are there triffids coming at me from all directions?' The bindweed, the bramble, the dock, the creeping buttercup, grew at a pace I'd previously not thought possible.

Normally they're bad enough, but gardeners get into a system. You learn to judge how to deal with weeds, just enough to keep them at bay and stop them setting seed for next year. In 2012 they were on steroids. Just as the 2012 Olympics seemed relatively free of drug cheats*, our gardens were experiencing a festival of pumped-up steroid abuse. Rangy brambles in Cornish hedgerows reached for the stars like cranes on a Newquay skyline. You could remove all the rosebay willow herb from a flowerbed one weekend, and by the following weekend more would have taken their place, already two feet tall, standing there bold as you like, saying *"Come on then, if you think you're hard enough!"* The weeds of 2012 defied all the laws of gravity, nature, and decency. The summer of 2012 was when everything changed in the garden. It was unsettling. It was just plain scary.

I suppose it was the combination of a colossal amount of rain with the occasional hour or two of proper hot sunshine that did it. Not nearly enough sun to placate a family of four who've shelled out a grand and a half for a week in a cottage with sea glimpses, but easily enough to get your average weed sprinting at the sun as if it was the last chance it was ever going to get. Which it pretty much was. In theory, grazing animals had more grass to eat than normal, but they couldn't get to it because the fields had become bogs.

By the end of the summer we were cheerfully informed that a billion pounds had been knocked off the UK economy, thanks to cancelled events and spoilt crops. And in Cornwall I'd say we felt it more keenly than a lot of places.

So I'm afraid this year I've abandoned my usual cheerful British triumph-of-hope-over-experience attitude. It may not be quite as bad as last year, but I bet it's not far off. I am resigned to the painful spectre of a summer in long trousers, without sun, or any hope of a barbecue, or any pleasure, at all, ever. The thing is, if you expect nothing you're not going to be disappointed.

Vans

2016

Y ou may remember some time ago my suggesting that if you want to look the part in Cornwall, there's nothing more Cornish than a beaten-up, dirty old estate car. Now although this stands true, I feel compelled to share with you a comparatively recent revelation: these days, where I live, practically everyone seems to drive a van.

I don't mean a small, car-sized van. Nor do I mean a hugely valuable, classic *VW Combi* campervan, so beloved of *Channel 4* stylists attempting to show Jamie Oliver-type TV presenters being all young and carefree (the irony being that the purchase price and maintenance of such a classic vehicle necessitates a sizable disposable income). No, I'm talking about the kind of van that we used to always generically refer to as a *Ford Transit*. The drivers of these vans aren't builders, or delivery drivers, or holidaymakers. They're people going about their daily Cornish lives. I tell you, if you want to look like a local in 21st century Cornwall, you need a geet big van. I know people who wouldn't be seen driving anything else. You hear stories of the school run upcountry, where you simply have to drive a Chelsea tractor. Where I live, that doesn't exist.

I wasn't aware of this phenomenon when I was growing up. Not that there weren't any vans – in fact I spent all of the sixties and much of the seventies in the back of my dad's Truro pram shop delivery van (an *Austin A50*, as I recall). How us kids would jostle for prime position, perched on one of the two available rock-hard rear wheel arches (never mind seat belts – we didn't even have *seats*). Then, upon passing my driving test in 1980, the shop van (by now a 1976 *Morris Marina*) was my main set of wheels. Although it was deeply uncool (*'Rickards Prams and Toys, Truro'* written on the side, with a smiley, waving cartoon jester), it was a lot better than walking.

Back then, only a very small minority seemed to be driving a van as a 'lifestyle choice'. A big reason for this relatively modern deluge of vans has to be surf culture. Whereas we used to just strap our boards on the roof of our cars (well, until the eighties anyway, when surfboards became small enough to fit *inside* our cars), in a van you can have the luxury of transporting them easily and securely. But you also have somewhere to get changed, warm up, and generally hang out. You can fit them out for camping, you can chuck pretty much anything in the back, you can crash out in them after a party. Oh there are lots of things you can do in a van. Above all, a van says 'I'm a surfer'.

You can guess what's coming. I held out for fifteen years. I loved our (t)rusty old estate car, even if it was starting to feel decidedly claustrophobic. But by the time my kids were seven, their bikes were getting big, and so was our collection of camping gear. Annual camping trips to France were becoming an increasingly loathsome logistical exercise, and I was developing a full-blown phobia of sand and mud. Then, overnight, I realised that all of our transportation issues could be solved for the foreseeable future, simply by trading in our estate, and getting something bigger.

And so, a little reluctantly, we joined the van club. Actually we don't even qualify as the lowliest of members, because it's not a cool German one – I'm much too cheap to stump up that kind of cash. In fact it's distinctly uncool, but I like it that way. Our modest French version does everything we need. It's got no carpet for sand and mud to get stuck in. It's got seats in the back for the kids to sit on, and windows for them to look through. It's surprisingly nimble, and only a few inches longer than the estate was. Best of all, it's swallowed everything we've thrown at it so far: children, bikes, surfboards, camping gear...

Of course it has. That's the point. It's a van. And vans are great. I should have got one years ago.

Gooseyphobia

2006

W e've had our geese six years now. You may recall Audrey's broken leg from a couple of years ago. The pin seems to have done its job, and you'd only know there had ever been a problem when you notice her limping slightly in cold weather. Dear of her. Audrey and her four friends have become part of the family, and we love them. But it seems not everyone does.

People have strong feelings about geese. When anyone comes and meets ours for the first time, they generally say one of two things. They either say "Apparently geese make very good guard dogs don't they? Guard geese!" Or they say something like "Whoa... I'm very wary of geese 'cause I was chased by some when I was young". Sometimes they say both.

I've got a bit of a problem with both of these statements. Granted, geese do like to make a noise when they see something unfamiliar. That distinctive hoarse honking is their way of alerting their pals of the threat of danger, not to mention the possibility of a feeding opportunity. They might even walk or trot towards you with their neck outstretched, just to say hello. But, unless it's the breeding season, they're extremely unlikely to try and make contact with you. And if they do, it would only be the gander, protecting his girls.

As far as I can remember, this has only happened once in six years, right in the middle of the breeding season, when my friend Les visited. He's the kind of thrill-seeking, outdoorsy type who positively enjoys the sight of a twenty pound goose coming at him, hissing. He'd be thinking to himself something along the lines of "Hmm, I wonder if this is going to hurt as much as when I hit the rocks in that seven foot shorebreak at Gwithian yesterday. Let's find out".

So Captain Beaky kept coming, and Les held his ground. The mighty orange serrated beak clamped onto Les' shin, and Les looked down, fascinated. Captain Beaky looked up, as if to say "There. That'll teach you not to run away when I hiss at you". And Les peered down at him, as if to say "Is that it? You haven't even got my skin. That's my jeans".

And that's about as bad as it ever gets when one of our geese is in attack mode. Poor Captain Beaky tried the same thing with a fox a month later and found this new predator rather less forgiving than my friend had been. He became our only fox victim in six years. We've gone from one extreme to the other as we have a new gander now, Gordon, who seems confused about his sexuality. Hence the name. But that's another story. The point is, our geese are good guard dogs in that they make a bit of a racket when they see somebody, but they're not exactly up there with a Doberman Pinscher.

As for everyone's story about childhood goose chases, I think it's nothing more than gooseyphobia. We've all been chased by a dog at some point, haven't we? Most of us have been chased by them lots of times, throughout our childhood.

Possibly even bitten. But how many of us are scared of dogs as a result? Not that many. So what have we all got against geese? I think it's gooseyphobic hogwash, fuelled partly by hazy memories of youth, and also the fact that canned goose fat seems to be enjoying a renaissance in fashionable roasting pans nationwide, so it helps if you don't get too attached to them (needless to say I've long since abandoned any kind of Hugh Fearnley-Whittingstall approach to my goose husbandry. I do admit that it crossed my mind to use Captain Beaky's post-fox-attack-virtually-unscathed-carcass for a nice roast, but when it came to it, it seemed about as likely as casseroling the family moggy. So I spent two hours digging a hole in a nice corner of our rock-hard field for him. The fox came back that night and dug him up again for a late supper anyway).

I will admit that geese seem to have a problem with wheels. They love to go for anything on wheels. Bicycles, wheel-barrows and postpeople's vans are all fair game to a goose, for some reason. Red rags to a bull. They're not too keen on hosepipes either. But generally speaking, our geese are amiable, vegetarian, inquisitive, useful pets, and a delight to have around. And if you don't agree, come round here, and I'll set the geese on you. You'll like it.

Flat leaf parsley

2016

I recently stumbled upon a rather annoying article on a national broadsheet's website, in which the writer sought to enlighten us as to how laughably inferior old-fashioned parsley is. You know, the curly stuff. I had no idea! I may have been vaguely aware that you see a lot more of the flat leaf version around these days, but I hadn't quite grasped just how out-of-style curly parsley had become. Apparently if you're still stupid enough to use it as a garnish, it's symptomatic of 'a dish that's retro', and 'a cook who has run out of ideas...' Heavens. I feel such a fool for ever having set eyes on the wretched stuff. It's definitely flat leaf parsley all the way for me now. Shame I've got a massive cushion of the curly version growing happily right outside the kitchen. If only I'd known how completely useless and retro it is.

We Brits are great at this. We love being the one to exclaim, "What were we thinking – it's *these* ones we should be eating!" It's the same with walnuts, I'm told. You can't eat manky old dried walnuts in 2016! You have to eat the fresh ones. Obviously I've revised my monthly order with *Fortnum's*.

This constant need for reinvention isn't confined to food, but also applies to the serving of it. I remember well over a decade ago at the Porthminster Beach Café, thinking what a funky idea it was to keep the wine cool in a jaunty, children's plastic beach bucket. But it's got out of hand. These days, we don't bat an eyelid when our lunch is served to us on a plank of wood. I recently ordered rhubarb crumble for pudding and the rhubarb was placed on one end of the plank, served in a storage jar complete with lid, and the actual crumble bit was down the other end, in a neat little pile. It tasted great, but I found it hard to chew with my mouth contorted into an incredulous sneer.

I thought it was bad enough before that when perfectly functional, circular plates morphed, overnight, into a square shape, for no obvious reason at all (other than to perhaps test the mettle of the poor washer upper). I dare say it'll get worse before it gets better. Let's see...soup served in a bedpan? Chips poking out of a pair of vintage Dunlop Green Flash, the vinegar in a teensy porcelain thimble?

Here's the thing though. Just as I remain unconvinced about the superiority of flat leaf parsley, or dinner on a plank, so I was about Jerusalem artichokes. I loathed the things, and that loathing has been well documented on this page. I thought that their advocates were the same deluded fashion victims who probably considered plank food and flat leaf parsley as the only way to live. The emperor's new clothes, I said. But I have experienced a culinary epiphany. Those people were right, and I was wrong. I've just roasted some Jerusalem artichokes (I'm not really sure why), and now I'm eating them along with a side dish of humble pie, because I accidentally left them in for longer than planned, and something rather wonderful

happened. They turned all pulpy in the middle, anc
went all chewy, almost caramelised, and the whole thing
sweet, smoky revelation.

My conclusion is obvious: I need to be a bit less judgmental. Broaden my horizons. I never thought bottled water would catch on once the novelty wore off, but people still buy it for some reason. It's becoming increasingly apparent to me that many of these things are not passing fads at all. Just because I haven't yet grasped the benefits of food on a plank, doesn't mean there aren't any. I just have to keep an open mind, and wait for further enlightenment.

Cupcakes though. What on *earth* is that about?

Twitcher

2007

T witcher. It's one of those words people chuck about with abandon whenever they see an opportunity. How often do you read in the paper something along the lines of: *'Twitchers celebrate good year for tawny owls'*. But they do not mean *twitcher*. They mean people interested in birds. Bird-watchers. Or, to use the more modern word, *birders*. A real twitcher would not actually be all that interested in tawny owls. Here's why.

You can be happily in conversation with a twitcher, when all of a sudden they'll stare off into the middle distance, completely distracted by some barely perceptible little squeak from the undergrowth, twitching and cocking their head, binoculars tightly grasped, to be raised as soon as an unfamiliar little brown thing is spotted hopping about in the undergrowth. "Definitely a Cetti's warbler," they might say. "Haven't seen one since that female in '98."

That's a twitcher. An extreme birdwatcher. Obsessive types who are constantly in search of a new and unusual species. The relatively common tawny owl is of little interest to the twitcher, assuming they've already ticked it off their list. Twitchers are the ones you read about going to Scilly every October, rushing from island to island, checking their lists and getting all excited just because some poor migrant, in all likelihood common as muck in its usual part of the world, has ended up in this, a foreign country. Twitchers celebrate this, the sighting of a bird which is, arguably, a bit rubbish. It's probably not that rare, and it's probably not that bright. Let's face it, the particular bird they're looking at is lost. It isn't exactly a shining example of the species – it's the one who got it a bit wrong, the one who was heading north, sliced it a bit to the right and arrived here knackered, hungry, confused and lonely.

Nice people though, twitchers. I come across quite a few due to the fact that I'm a chough watch volunteer, and a lot of people come to see the choughs not because our gorgeous, mystical and sacred bird has returned to its homeland, but simply because it is rare here in Cornwall, and therefore is very 'tickable offable'. To coin a technical term.

I remember a few years ago, whilst walking with friends one Sunday afternoon at Loe Bar, I had a first hand encounter with twitchers. We'd stopped to watch a funny little wading bird that was messing about in a small pond. My bird knowledge was nowhere near good enough to put a name to the little chap, but my friends and I were all quite sure we hadn't seen one before, because of its bright yellow legs. It wasn't doing much, so we looked at it for a bit, scratched our heads and then carried on walking back to the car. Like you do. And then the first twitcher arrived. A youngish man, all in green military gear, binoculars around neck, telescope on a pole over his shoulder, mobile phone in hand. Evidently mistaking us for people in the know due to our disheveled, rustic appearance, the presence of anoraks and muddy boots, his eyes narrowed to slits as he asked, rather urgently, "*Have you seen it?*"

"What's that then?" we replied, a little taken aback.

"Lesser Yellowlegs. I got a report of a sighting in one of these pools." There was a pause, and then, obviously disappointed and a little embarrassed he said, "You're not twitchers, are you?"

"No," we replied. "We just, er, got lucky." It transpired that this man had travelled from north Devon to see the little bird. We were pleased to have had the mystery creature identified, and pointed the man in the right direction. After that as we carried on along the path the twitchers started coming thick and fast. At first I thought we were being helpful by calmly and concisely greeting any likely looking new arrival with succinct directions before they had a chance to even ask. "Lesser Yellowlegs?" we'd say. "Two hundred yards, second pool on your left." I thought that would be the sort of pared-down factual approach these people would appreciate. But then we started to realise from their irritated expression that they didn't want this; they wanted to find it for themselves, or at least search until they came upon a large group of drooling soulmates all leaning over a hedge together, eyes trained on a small, brown and completely oblivious little bird. So we said nothing from then on.

It's easy to be flippant about twitchers. It's easy to say, "If you want to see an American robin, go to America. There's plenty". Our society loves to mock any kind of obsessive person, especially if they like to spot things, or collect things. We call them *anoraks*. But at least they're interested in something. Better than that, they are experts in something. And experts are people who get things done in life. In their quest for knowledge they discover things, and invent things, and go places. I envy them. I'm not an expert at anything; I simply don't have the attention span. So I say hats off to the twitcher.

One Cornwall

2009

So, on April Fool's Day our much-heralded Cornish Unitary Authority Superduper Council Thingy officially takes off. I've no idea whether it's a good idea or not as it's all a bit complicated. I'm much more concerned about what their new logo looks like. Like many people a few weeks ago, I was hopping mad and champing at the bit to throw in my three penneth about how daft their proposed idea was. It wasn't *change* I was afraid of *per se*, even though we may as well admit that we're all programmed to fear change (unless change means Obama replacing Bush of course. There can't be many people in the world who think *that* change is a bad idea). No, it was definitely the logo itself that was getting to me.

I had to be careful, because I remember initially not liking the 2012 Olympic logo, and then it kind of grew on me, and now I almost think it's OK. But this was never going to happen with the council's silly yellow-and-black bonfire effort. It was just so bland. Yes, I could see how the colours were *our* colours, and yes, I could just about make out a St Piran's Cross in there if I squinted. But that really was about it.

Now designing a logo is not rocket science. The graphic design world is festooned with stories about now famous logos that were happened upon, or scribbled hastily on the back of a fag packet in the pub, minutes before the deadline. Surely they could do better than this.

What had really tipped me over the edge was watching a patronising video on the council's website which showed us what the new logo would look like printed on stationery, vans and signs, as if the very sight of the thing *in situ* would make we Cornish sceptic dullards see the light, realise how naïve we'd been, crying out in unison: "Now I see how a cartoony stylised yellow and black bonfire is the perfect logo for us! It's just...so...Cornish!" Ooh, that did get my back up.

The council's bragging about how great their efforts were didn't help. They claimed the logo was *'inspiring and dynamic, bringing a contemporary modern feel to the best of Cornish tradition,'* and that the *'positive, dynamic lines of the design represent growth and movement'*. Good grief.

So I took my place in the long line of seething Cornishfolk, and like thousands of others I signed the petition, and whined to everyone about the absurdity of how an in-house team could come up with this logo, get it approved by an in-house committee, then present it to a public who then refused to roll over meekly and have their bellies branded with this generic symbol, instead of something real and tangible. It just wasn't right. It felt like yet another example of stealth diminution of our Cornish identity by the government machine. Further denial of the fact that we're not just another county.

The Radio Cornwall phone-in was busier than ever. Blogging was frenzied. Horns were locked. Lines were clearly drawn between those superannuated, index-linked, half-of-them-probably-not-even-born-here, jobs-for-life, closed-shop, pen-pushing civil servants, and a rabid, vocal minority of Kernewek-chanting, Mebyon Kernow-voting, set in their ways, living in the past and damn well gonna stay there, fearing change in all its manifestations, pasty-munching Cornish, all of whom wanted to keep the old logo. I'm generalising a little, obviously.

So what happened? Something amazing, that's what. After all the unrest, a group called the *One Cornwall Implementation Executive* decided at the end of January to revert to the old logo. Not the one with the miner and fisherman, just the version with the bezants and chough. On the website that day the rather contrite council boss gave the reason: 'Some members of the public continue to be unhappy with the design'.

So this month I'm not whingeing. I'm celebrating. But I'm also asking, what are we to make of it all? What conclusion is there to be drawn? Well, there's an obvious one I can think of. Sometimes perhaps we just have to admit it. Cornwall may be changing fast. But we're still, deep down, a bit of an old-fashioned sort of place.

Beer

2013

When I turned eighteen, I couldn't have timed it worse, beer-wise. It was 1980, and beer quality in Cornwall was at an all-time low. Our dads had all abandoned the Double Diamond of the seventies and fallen victim to something just as bad: a fashion for cold, fizzy continental lager.

In 1980, as far as I can remember, there were only two breweries in the entire county. The first, St Austell, was all right. Their pubs all had seductive black-and-gold livery, and their *Hicks Special Draught*, (HSD or 'High Speed Death' as we called it) was strong stuff, and most appealing to an 18-year-old eager to live life on the edge. But alas, St Austell pubs were few and far between. More common were Devenish ones, with insipid green and gold signage, and disappointing beer to match. Thus my mates and I weened ourselves on Devenish's very ordinary 'Cornish' bitter. Yep, that was its name. Its taste was about as ambitious. True, it cost less than 50p a pint, but there was just something plain depressing about it all.

Sure enough, Devenish pubs dwindled until soon they disappeared altogether. We were now destined to spend those oh-so-important formative pub years drinking some pretty depressing offerings. Many was the time you'd go into a pub and be forced to drink something pretending to be proper ale, brought in kegs from some vast factory upcountry, dispensed from a little electric tap on the bar, invariably with a name like 'Saxon' (which, to be honest, would have looked more appropriate on a machine in the Gents).

I was soon to discover that the demise of decent beer wasn't confined to Cornwall. Moving to London in 1985 I experienced an event so grim that it was to turn me away from ale altogether for the next few years. I was in a Covent Garden pub and got served a pint of bitter so rancid that I immediately complained to the barman. He looked me in the eye, refused to change it, and in all seriousness, swore that it was supposed to taste like that.

But then in the nineties everything changed, and nowhere more so than in Cornwall. Who could possibly have predicted such a revolution? Well, maybe Bill Sharp did, when he set up Sharp's near Rock in 1994. Or the Skinners, who started up in Truro shortly after. And now, thanks to such pioneers, we're awash with divine ale. Expensive, but divine. There are now around a couple of dozen breweries in Cornwall, including one on Scilly. It's fantastic. Lovely people, doing something they love, to produce something we all love. I winced two years ago when Sharp's (who must be given credit for kicking this whole thing off) was bought by one of the biggest breweries in the world: Molsen Coors. But benefits come with such an acquisition; the sheer clout of this giant is enabling all Cornish beers to reach whole new levels of recognition and credibility (personally I'd always choose a pint of Skinner's Betty Stogs over a pint of Sharp's Doom Bar anyway).

Cornish beer, completely unknown a couple of decades ago, is seriously on the map now. I just returned from a trip to London, and I found its availability quite shocking. There were familiar-looking Cornish pumps on the bar of four out of the five pubs I entered (Whitechapel, Broadgate, Tooting and Kennington – a reasonable geographical spread). Doom Bar is so ubiquitous in London that my Kennington friend refused a pint of it, protesting that he could drink it any old time, and that he'd 'prefer to try one of their guest beers'.

Who'd have thought. In the Dickens Inn I sat down with my brother, who lives in London, but was born and raised in Cornwall like me. He had a pint of Doom Bar, and I had a pint of Fuller's London Pride. We took a sip. Both were perfect: fresh, clear, and pumped up from the cellar through lovely clean pipes. We exchanged glances, and knew exactly what each other was thinking.

We took another sip, and we laughed.

Demelza's crawlers

2016

C rikey. I've just realised it's been six months since I last
mentioned *Poldark* on this page. I distinctly remember
vowing to bring the subject up whenever possible, in order to
help alleviate the agony of waiting for the second series to
begin. This time last year, series one was almost upon us. But it
looks as if we're going to have to wait a while for the much-
anticipated series two to air, so I feel that it's particularly
pressing that we talk about it some more.

Let's be positive – the longer we wait, the better it'll be. And
at least this second series is going to be two episodes longer, so
that's all good. Also good is the fact that last year's series is still
entertaining us in unexpected ways. For example, it's
unwittingly brought at least two very useful new expressions
into my household.

Firstly, there's *the putrid throat*. Don't get me wrong – I
certainly wouldn't want to make light of actual diphtheria (to
give *the putrid throat* its modern name). It's a truly awful, not to
mention fatal, disease, thankfully now drastically diminished
due to widespread vaccination. But with kids at primary
school in 2016 I find it endlessly amusing to use the term to
describe, well, virtually any ailment. "Tom's off with a horrid
cold," said a playground mum to me just the other day. "Ah," I

replied dramatically, exaggerating my accent. "The ol' *putrid throat* eh?"

Well, I think it's funny anyway. Interestingly, Winston Graham only called it a rather more generic *'the sore throat'* (yes, I've just checked in one of my wife's many copies of *Demelza*). While *Poldark* screenwriter Debbie Horsfield stayed impressively true to the original books, her *putrid throat* tweak is a neat little example of her art, and how something so subtle can be so effective.

Another useful word from last year's *Poldark* is *'crawlers'*. So much more graphic than 'head lice'. Not that anyone in my house has ever had crawlers, you understand. Ross's eighteenth century plan of attack in combatting the odious arthropods entrenched in Demelza's otherwise perfect scalp is very different to ours. These days, most people spend the best part of twenty quid on a bottle of acrid, flammable, oily, chemical solution, apply it to their child's hair, divide the scalp into carefully measured transects, comb it through methodically with a teensy weensy little comb for an hour, wash it out, let them walk around in plain view for a couple of days with hair that looks like it's been doused with *WD40*, then repeat the process days later, only to find that the vile little creatures are still in there. Laughing. So I'm told.

Demelza's obviously in a bad way. Prudie takes one look at her upon her arrival at Nampara and announces her diagnosis from ten yards: "She be seethin' with crawlers!" But just as Dwight Enys was not yet able to provide an efficacious diphtheria vaccination, there was no *Superdrug* to furnish

113

sufferers with an effective nit treatment. So what does Ross do? Simply sticks Demelza's offending locks under the pump in the yard, drenches her with freezing water, has a bit of a rummage, and hopes for the best. Demelza's crawlers are not mentioned again, so we can only surmise that Cap'n Poldark's delousing techniques are more effective than they look. And considerably more efficient than his scything.

Talking of which, at the time of writing, the infamous scything scene has just been voted TV moment of 2015 by *Radio Times* readers. Apparently it drew a whopping 45% of the votes, followed by a *Strictly Come Dancing* performance, and a monologue from *Doctor Who*. I'm a stranger to teatime celebrity dancing shows and children's science fiction, so I'm really not qualified to say. Personally the scything scene left me cold. My vote would probably have gone to the scene in which Zacky Martin stuffs it to the Warleggans at the auction.

Well, that's about enough *Poldark* for now. I realise that me waffling on here is a measly substitute for a fresh new glimpse of Aidan Turner. But I've done me best.

Rad dad

2011

I n 1977 I was a Truro skateboarder. I don't mean I did a bit
of skateboarding, as in a hobby. It was my world. On non-
schooldays, once I'd finished my paper round at 8am, and if I
wasn't working anywhere else, I lived, breathed, ate, and slept
skateboards. Skateboarding's popularity went through the roof
in the late seventies, and it was probably the only time in my
life that I've been at the very heart of the zeitgeist.

My friends and I doodled the logos of all the American
skateboard companies constantly. I learned them so well I can
still draw them now. We knew the name of every professional
Californian skateboarder the way a kid from Manchester
would probably have reeled off footballers. All my money
went on skate gear (which was horrifically expensive before
they started importing it in quantity from the US).

At first we kids would gather on the big council car park at
the back of Hardy Carpets. Any sort of municipal skateboarding facility was unthinkable, partly because no-one knew
if this rapidly growing craze would last. When the councillors
threw us off the car park, we'd skate wherever we could. We
never got into any serious trouble, but we got shouted out by
old men, and on more than one occasion had our names taken
by the police. My dad hated me skateboarding: *"Going out to*

play on your skateboard again then?" he'd tut as I went off to indulge in the only sport at which I would ever excel.

Then a skatepark opened in Watergate Bay. Its surface was rough and it seemed to have its banks in all the wrong places, but we loved it. This makeshift mecca was the only place we wanted to be that hot summer, and we'd scramble to get to Watergate any way we could, cadging lifts from absolutely anyone. We'd skate from dawn til dusk. We got good too, and by the time more facilities started opening (the Flamingo in Pool, converted from the old dance hall, and then a much bigger, proper concrete skatepark at Holywell Bay), we'd sometimes be collared to represent local teams in contests.

One day in late '78 I broke my leg at Holywell, attempting a newly-discovered aerial manoeuvre, and spent 8 weeks in a full plaster cast. By the time I was fully functional again it was winter, and quite a few of us had moved on. People were starting to talk about college options, and things were never quite the same again. Then some of us started passing driving tests, so we could more easily get to the beach, and, predictably, surfing took over.

These days, skateboarding is a colossal global street culture. Tony Hawk, skateboarding's greatest celebrity, is widely considered one of the world's most influential athletes. And now every village seems to have a skateboard facility of some kind, and the one at Hendra in Truro is nothing short of fabulous. I genuinely feel pangs of envy for the Truro skaters who have access to such a wondrous place.

And now I can't stop thinking about picking up a skateboard again. The itch never leaves you. But forever cursed by the antisocial stigma, and haunted by my dad's words, I can't imagine I'd ever do it again in any serious way. Not at my age. There's something plain odd about a forty-nine-year-old man riding a skateboard.

That is, until now. Finally I think the day may have arrived, for two reasons: *1)* I've discovered I'm not alone. I read an article recently about '*The Rise of the Rad Dad*'. These are middle-aged men, just like me, who are picking up their boards again, and going skateboarding with their kids (at well managed facilities, of course). There's even a web forum. *2)* As I approach fifty, I'm starting to care less about what anyone thinks of me. I've still got a couple of boards in the garage, and they're looking a lot more tempting than a set of golf clubs.

So, if you spot any conspicuously grey-haired old men on skateboards out there, it might be wise to give them a wide berth – it could be the first time they've been on that thing for thirty years.

Down the Mennaye

2012

There we were, Graham and me, down the Mennaye, one damp 'n' drizzly Bank Holiday Monday in May, and it was all a bit tense. After the bittersweet thrill of narrowly missing out on winning the RFU Championship the previous season, the Cornish Pirates were now embarking on the first leg of this season's playoffs. Our opponent today was Bristol, a team who'd won 17 out of 22 games this season, finished way ahead, and were hot favourites for promotion. "It's gonna be close," said Graham, through gritted teeth. The TV cameras were there, Falmouth Marine Band did their best to take our minds off our knotted bellies, and the atmosphere built.

After ten minutes, Bristol had exposed gaping holes in our defence, converted two tries, and were 14 - 0 ahead. Their players re-assembled on the halfway line and prepared to ramp up a big score. We steeled ourselves for a beating. And then a lovely thing happened.

A small, unruly flock of herring gulls appeared from the Penzance end, and cruised nonchalantly towards the centre of the pitch. Then, cocky as you like, they flew right over the Bristol players. As they did so, one bird dipped down so low that I swear it could only have been a foot above the Bristol captain's head.

Now, I'd love to spin some yarn about a naughty gull leaving a deposit on the captain's head, or pecking the hooker on the nose after which he became so unnerved that he never regained his composure, thus forfeiting the game. But those things didn't happen. Obviously.

Those gulls flying over the Bristol players had no idea what was going on below. They didn't see a local team 14 - 0 down against a squad of men who had travelled here for this sole purpose. It never occurred to the gulls that the sight of three thousand people around the edge of a big rectangle of grass, watching thirty muddy ones running around, chasing after an oval ball, and bumping into each other a lot, was unusual.

They were oblivious to the fact that this was arguably the most hallowed rugby ground in a county for whom rugby is the one true sport. No, the one thing those gulls thought was the thing gulls always think: *"There's a gathering of people over there. Let's go and check it out. There may be chips"*.

Those gulls had no idea that these thirty men were athletes at the top of their game, whose minds couldn't have been further from eating chips (gulls may be bright, but they're not that bright). I just love that nature doesn't give a damn. And the herring gull has honed not giving a damn to a fine art.

Of course, my brain not being the sharpest, and the rugby being a bit depressing, I let my mind wander, and watched those gulls. I watched as they concluded that no chips were to be had here today, and swept off seawards over the main stand, still on the lookout for the next likely meal. An overflowing bin on the seafront, more than likely. Good luck to them. The herring gull: Cornwall's most beautiful yet misunderstood hero.

Ah, but what of the final score, I hear you ask. Well, we came back in spectacular fashion, and won 45 - 24. It was as impressive a performance as I've ever seen the Pirates put on, and certainly the comeback of the season. On the radio afterwards they were saying that it had been an inspired spectacle in which every Pirates player was at the very top of his game.

I'd never claim that the cheeky gull flyby had anything to do with the dramatic change in the Pirates' fortunes that day. Then again, the bird lover in me likes to think that perhaps the visiting side found the approach of a flock of the most important birds in Cornwall, scavengers with beaks like sharpened clawhammers, a little unsettling. Probably not, since Bristol has a massive gull population too.

Either way though, makes you think.

2012

2012

Oh my. That was ridiculous.

2012 I mean. It really was all a bit bonkers wasn't it? At the very least it was far, far more eventful than your average year. In a good way. Forget about the mind numbingly awful summer. Forget the fact that the country plummeted even deeper into a seemingly endless recession. Things happened this year that genuinely made us forget all the misery and collectively scream: "Yes! This....is....*great!*"

Now, I have no recollection of the Golden Jubilee ten years ago, other than a vague memory of Brian May playing a tortuous guitar solo on a very windy roof in a very flappy coat. But the Diamond one this year took us all by surprise. It's the most well worn cliché in the book, but it really did bring communities together to celebrate in a tangible way. I say 'celebrate'. I'm confident that a good number of us weren't that bothered that we've had the same monarch for sixty years, but the point is that we got together, and it was fun. And the terrible weather enhanced it, sort of, making it all seem somehow more appropriate. More British. It showed the world that in Blighty it takes more than days and days of torrential rain to dampen our spirits. It gave the Queen the chance to show us what she's made of too – an old lady stoically bracing herself on the slippery deck of that rain-lashed barge for hours on end, without so much as batting an expensively powdered eyelid. As for her husband, he did the same but with a bladder infection. The next day as he was admitted to hospital, you could hear the nation shout in unison, "Respect, Sir!" Best of all, I definitely spotted some Cornish pilot gigs in among that vast flotilla on the Thames.

The Golden Jubilee was quite a do at the time, but soon seemed a fleeting trifle as the Olympics approached. We Cornish were first to catch on, when at 7am on 19th May our own Ben Ainslie picked up the torch at Lands End. By the end of that first day it was in Plymouth and the Cornish were fully on board (that is, apart from those in the Camborne/Redruth area, who were curiously bypassed. We never did get a satisfactory explanation for that). We all seemed to know someone involved (the missus got to carry the torch in St Austell – a day we'll never forget), and it felt surprisingly personal. It was as if we Cornish had had first dibs, and now we owned it. From then on, whenever the torch popped up on the news as it traversed the UK, we'd say, "We had it first!"

Any vestiges of scepticism disappeared as soon as the opening ceremony began. This was a theatrical event of such scale and ambition that I'd be amazed if we ever look upon anything remotely like it again in our lifetime. Conceived and directed for a global TV audience by a brilliant film director, we sat and stared at hours of stunning, mad, hilarious, seamlessly executed, quintessentially British spectacle. Then the Olympics and Paralympics themselves surpassed any of our expectations. It was all so impeccably well run. The naysayers shut their mouths early on. Heroes were born on a practically hourly basis. Cornishpeople were right up there. A modest girl from Penzance won the very first gold medal for Britain. Tom Daley (oh come on, he's from Plymouth – we're having a bit of him) won a bronze medal and it was every bit as good as any gold medal because it was unbelievably hard (he'd lost his dad and gained a ridiculous number of A levels during the previous year. Some boy). Ben Ainslie won gold. Again. There were so many surprises. We were left gazing upon it all, scratching our heads as if to say, "OK, so we can do such things in this country. We just have to believe it".

And now we're gearing up for the start of 2013. All I can say is thank goodness for 2012. We needed it.

Drummer

2008

There's an old, but rather good, joke about drummers in bands being thick, which I won't tell here for fear of causing offence. Besides, I'm sure their reputation isn't deserved. Drummers in bands often have a far more integral role than we ever give them credit for. Ringo's *Octopus's Garden* might not have been the Fab Four's finest hour, but they wouldn't have been the Beatles without him. Led Zeppelin's drummer John Bonham was such a vital part of the band that they split up soon after he died in 1980.

And I've always had a soft spot for Queen's drummer, Roger Taylor, ever since an urban myth did the rounds at Truro School in the seventies. The story went that Mr Taylor, an ex-pupil, was invited to come back to take part in the school's centenary celebrations. He was reputed to have told them where to go as he couldn't stand the place. With hindsight, I doubt the story's true, but he found a place in many a Truro schoolboy's heart that day.

Obviously most members of bands are cool, but I've always had a particular regard for the drummer. Drummers are great: Keith Moon, Animal from the Muppet Show, that gorilla in the chocolate ad. The fact is, many of us fancy ourselves as drummers. I know I always have. But sadly in truth the only time I've ever even had a go on some drums was in the school brass band hut one lunchtime when the bandmaster was unexpectedly detained at the doctor's. Such unforeseen absences were much relished, since they presented us bored young cornet and euphonium players with the opportunity to have a bash on other people's instruments. And the drumkit was the holy grail when it came to having a bash. The noise I made didn't quite match the polished sound I'd planned in my head, but I was sure I'd be quite brilliant at it with a bit of practice. We all think that about the drums. Like driving. We all have a subliminal assumption that we are, innately, a better driver than the next person. So it is with the drums. We all fancy our chances. Well I do anyway.

Which explains this bit of interesting news. Sales of drum kits have doubled since 2000, reaching an enormous £41 million last year. And apparently it's middle-aged men like me who are getting them. Just think, cheaper than a Harley Davidson, but just as loud and rebellious, and unlike a Harley you don't have to worry about it raining, and you needn't feel at all self-conscious, because you're indulging yourself in private. And these days you don't even have to upset the neighbours with the awful racket, because you just get one of these new electronic drumkits so you can listen to yourself through headphones. How civilised is that!

There's an obvious reason for this latent population explosion of grey haired percussionists. It's because we're not embarrassed anymore, because our icons have never been this old before. With the Stones approaching their dotage, and the realisation that the strutting rock god of a few years ago is now waiting for his second heart bypass, you no longer feel like an old saddo.

Things are different these days. You feel about the right age for all this. Sure, your teenage grandson might laugh at you, but you just pity him for being born into an age when anonymous pop star drones are created on reality TV shows by comatose viewers who sadly don't seem to have anything better to do, and nobody listens to albums anymore because they don't have the attention span.

Rock and roll has been with us quite some time now, and the average age of a rocker has got higher and higher. So keep a straight face when the wife of your retired, mild-mannered next-door-neighbour lets on that her husband's bought a drumkit. Thrashing away in his garden shed on a Tuesday night is probably the most liberating thing he's ever done. He doesn't feel silly anymore. There's hope for the world. Besides, there's worse things he could be getting up to in there.

OK, I seem to have a little space left so here's that joke about drummers. But I don't mean it, OK? *A drummer in a rock band is fed up with everyone thinking he's stupid because he's just the drummer. Eventually he decides that if he's ever going to be taken more seriously he's going to have to learn to play the guitar instead. So he goes into the shop and says to the man: "I'm fed up with everyone thinking I'm an idiot just because I'm only the drummer. I'm not stupid, and I'm going to prove it. I want to learn the guitar. Please can you show me all the different ones?" To which the assistant replies, "Well, I would sir, but this is a fishmongers!"*

Lazy birder

2017

Well, it's happened. It's really happened. The realisation of a dream that began in 2001: Cornish choughs on my doorstep. OK not literally, obviously. But I've seen them a ten minute walk from my front door, which is close enough. Whether or not the plastic decoy chough that's been nailed to my garage roof for the past twelve years played any part in attracting them, I've no idea. But I like to think so.

I'll be the first to admit that I've been rather neglecting my responsibilities as an RSPB Chough Watch volunteer for some time now. Throughout the noughties I was out there on the Lizard's cliffs every spring, helping protect their nest. I even did night shifts. And I enjoyed nothing more than manning the telescope at the RSPB watchpoint at Southerly Point, helping the public share in the joy of witnessing the return of Cornwall's most special bird. It was brilliant.

But in recent years I've let things slide. Sure, I always keep an eye out when I'm ever on the Cornish coast path, but not in any official kind of role. It's not that the novelty's worn off – that's never going to happen for me – but life just seemed to get in the way.

Just lately though, things have hotted up dramatically for me, choughly speaking. Firstly, I was invited to read my chough-based children's book to my boys' class at school. Now, this was an emotional experience for me, regardless of whether or not the kids thought it was any good. When I wrote it eleven years ago, I didn't dare dream that I'd ever have a child to read it to. I didn't really know who I'd written the book for. I suppose I was just getting something out of my system.

Then, the very week I finished reading the last chapter to the class, I got a phone call. It was from a chough-loving friend in the next village. Keep an eye out for a pair of choughs, he said, right here over our local beach. They were part of a small group we know to be based a few miles up the coast, but now spreading their wings a bit. Apparently they'd been seen more than once on my bit of the coastline. I was instructed to survey it regularly and keep my eyes and ears open. So I did. It wasn't easy, because you have to walk right past my local bar on the beach in order to get to that bit of the coast path. Sometimes I went searching with my family, sometimes on my own. Always with a pair of binoculars. And I successfully managed to circumvent the alluring call of the ale, ignoring the bids of friends sitting on the pub's front sun terrace as I walked past.

"Come for a pint boy!"

"Can't!" I'd reply. "I'm looking for choughs!"

But I found nothing. OK, jackdaws, rooks, ravens, gulls, fulmars, guillemots, stonechats, pigeons and pipits. Which was nice. But no choughs. After a few weeks I let the doubts creep in. They were never going to come to me – it was simply too much to hope for. Then one evening last week I was doing the walk with a friend, and the call of the bar on the beach was too much. We didn't walk past. We went in. Just for a quick sundowner.

We sat out front, supping pints of Tribute and watching the sun disappear behind low-lying streaks of wispy cloud. And out of nowhere, there they were. Two choughs flying low, right past us. Unmistakable. No need to walk anywhere – they'd come to us.

"Choughs!" I exclaimed. "Definitely! Look!" It was fleeting; within seconds they'd disappeared around the next headland, heading east. We sat there, not quite believing what had just happened. I very nearly got up and followed them. But they were probably miles away by now. And we'd just got a fresh pint.

North/south divide

2012

T he *Office for National Statistics* recently published new figures for average life expectancy in the UK. "*Men in London can live up to fourteen years longer than their Glaswegian counterparts,*" proclaimed an eye-catching headline in *The Guardian*.

Now, while I'm sure we'd all much prefer life expectancy figures to be exactly equal throughout Britain, is this fourteen-year discrepancy really so surprising? It turns out that the Londoners being referred to are residents of an extremely well-heeled borough in south west London, where a fair proportion of the population are on six figure salaries and enjoying the pampered lifestyle and private healthcare that goes with it. Why should we be surprised that many residents of this pampered borough spend a champagne-and-oyster quaffing 85 years (and 87 for women) swanning about the boutiqueries of west London?

What is the point in comparing the most affluent place in the whole of Britain with a large city with its fair share of urban deprivation? Why not reverse the stats by comparing an affluent part of Glasgow with a deprived part of London? You might as well have a headline reading: '*Bananas are a Completely Different Shape to Oranges! And a Different Colour!*'

Articles like this invariably go on to make sweeping generalisations about the ever-widening 'north/south divide', an expression conjuring up visions of everyone south of the Watford gap living in six bedroom, detached, suburban houses, driving their 2.4 pony riding kids to prep school in their Range Rovers, while anywhere north of it is populated by unemployed Sun readers in squalid drug-addled sink estates idly watch their binge-drinking-asbo-tagged infants playing barefoot in burnt out Nissan Micras.

We Cornish generally scratch our heads in bemusement whenever we see the expression 'north/south divide'. The idea of some sort of horizontal line across Britain to denote affluence and poverty seems peculiar to us. Cornwall is in the south-west, not the south, and it feels very odd to be lumped into the same category as a part of Britain that is geographically as far from us as it is from Newcastle.

I can't deny that Cornwall has its share of wealth these days. People buy holiday cottages with sea glimpses for half a million a pop. On the surface the place is thriving. For many, Cornwall is just that place with the pretty beaches, and pasties, and pixies, and that nice Rick Stein. TV shows like Doc Martin exacerbate the false impression of a Cornish idyll by portraying the fictional fishing village of Portwenn, a place blissfully free of the vagaries of 21st century deprivation, where a dimwitted full-time policeman has nothing to do, and everyone lives in a lovely whitewashed cottage with a sea view.

Most of us know that the reality is very different. Cornwall is one of the poorest counties in Britain, with high unemployment, awful deprivation and salaries often half those in the south-east. North/south divide? No, it's just not like that.

I need to calm down. You're probably wondering where Cornwall sits on the life expectancy table. Well, rather pleasingly we're pretty much average for the UK. Men can expect to reach 78, while their wives get an extra four years. It seems quite appropriate, really. We're not Glasgow, and we're not west London.

And we're sure as hell not Portwenn.

Seasick

2014

Y ou may remember a couple of months ago I described
the most idyllic of times – a day's deep sea fishing trip
during last year's long, hot summer. The water was glassy, the
dolphins frolicked, the pollack, ling and gurnard were
plentiful, and above all, tummies were calm. It was heaven.
Since then, my group of friends speculated as to whether it
would be foolhardy to try and repeat such a perfect day.

Well, with open minds we did go out again, from
Newquay, this summer. Same boat, same skipper, eight of us
chaps, a year on. We fine-tuned the system a bit this time,
taking two cool boxes with us – one full of cold beer, one full of
warm pasties. The weather was nowhere near as nice, but it
was OK. "Let's just give it a go," we all agreed.

Leaving the harbour, it soon became evident that prevailing
westerlies were making the surface chop relentlessly
unforgiving. The boat was rolling all over the place, and there
was no escaping it. I've been out in such conditions enough
times to know what this was likely to mean. Sure enough,
within half an hour, two of our crew were turning a worrying
colour. I can't think of a word in the English language to
adequately describe the shade of grey that a deeply tanned face
turns as nausea sets in.

Reaching a reef a few miles out, we cut the engine. You can probably guess the rest. "How are you feeling?" I nervously asked my friend Bill. "Not great," he mumbled, sparingly, and with a substantial degree of understatement. Within minutes his sunglasses were tucked into his back pocket as he re-acquainted himself with his breakfast. Another half an hour and two more had joined him. It was 11.30am. We were supposed to be fishing til 5.30.

We able-bodied anglers fished on, keen to salvage something of the day and produce some bounty to throw on the evening's planned barbecue. But the atmosphere was less than ideal – it's hard to enjoy landing a 6lb Pollack, knowing that the man standing next to you has lost the will to live. And slowly, to differing degrees, we all fell. I've never felt remotely seasick in my life, but even my tummy was not as it should be.

I was aware that, as organiser of the trip, it was up to me to decide when to pack it in. On every fishing trip I've ever been on it's been generally accepted that the seasick have to grin and bear it, and not spoil it for the others. Which, to be honest, is pretty harsh, because it must be ghastly. And it can happen to anyone – it's common knowledge that Admiral Nelson frequently suffered.

What was I to do? Half of our party, though too public-spirited and brave to beg me to abort, were looking at me with an expression that can only be described as *pleading*. On the other hand, half of us were catching fish, and enjoying it, sort of. Several of us even managed to eat a pasty, though Geoff said hello again to his five minutes later.

In the end, a professional intervened. There happened to be a doctor on board, and it's when he said "I think we should call it a day, I can't watch these guys any longer," that we cut our losses, a couple of hours early. When we set foot on dry land, the cool boxes were barely any lighter than when we'd left.

An hour later and we were sitting outside the pub, downing pints of lovely brown beer, our euphoria enhanced by the realization that our other halves weren't expecting us back for another two hours. I dared broach the subject of doing it again next year. Maybe seasickness is a necessary evil, I suggested, the sort of awful experience you can get over, given time. Like childbirth.

At least four faces just stared back at me, blankly. As we dipped into the cool box and devoured the pasties, someone quietly said, "Have you ever heard the old Cornish saying: 'Never take a pasty on a boat' – it's really bad luck?" It rang a vague bell.

"Oh hell," I replied.

Visitor

2012

I t's amazing how an old house can become a part of you. I've lived in my old miner's cottage for thirteen years now. It was built in 1766 on Basset land, originally a little terrace of tiny, one-up-one-down cottages. Several generations of the same family lived in it for much of the 19th century, with Francis Basset, 1st Baron de Dunstanville (of Carn Brea monument fame) as their landlord.

The history is fascinating, but it's also a bit frustrating. Cottages like this were, by definition, no-frills and utilitarian, so there are surprisingly few clues left as to how the house was originally arranged. I'd love to know which room was used for what, or what it had looked like with a thatched roof. But this place was built to provide poor miners with shelter and warmth, because the alternative would have been living in a cave. So it wasn't exactly blessed with any original features worth saving. No fancy cornicing. No finely crafted feature mantelpieces either.

Granted, there are two roughly hewn original inglenook fireplaces that I'm sure haven't changed much. And I know the front garden used to be an orchard, and that there was a gate in the front hedge. I've found the evidence. But I crave more. For thirteen years I've fantasised about coming across someone old who could at least tell me what the house was like a few decades ago. That would be a start. But as the years have rolled by, I've come to terms with the realisation that I'd only ever get so far, that I was never going to find out more about this place which has become such a part of myself and my family.

Until last week.

Last week, a rather well dressed lady knocked on the kitchen door. At first I was nervous – she started backing away when I opened the door, muttering something about taking a picture of my house, and fumbling with something white in her hand. But then I heard her mention that she used to own the house, and hadn't set foot in it for fifty years. My jaw dropped. Then she presented me with two black and white photos she'd taken in the front garden in 1957. Oh, I thought, this is the big one. The Mothership. I'd waited all these years, and now I'd tapped into the main lode. My patience had been rewarded. I told her that I'd been waiting for her for thirteen years. Now it was her turn to feel nervous.

The stranger stayed for over an hour while I unleashed an unremitting deluge of detailed questions. I think she was a bit taken aback, but she rose to the challenge. She showed me where the Rayburn used to be, where there was once a trapdoor to access one of the upstairs bedrooms, where the orchard had been, even how there used to be an extra bedroom due to the altered position of the stairs. She described walking through the fields either side where bungalows have now sprung up. I listened, agog. It was just fantastic. Although this lady's personal experience went back less than a quarter of the cottage's history, it turned out that her *grandfather* had bought it at the beginning of the 20th century, directly from the Bassets!

She left, and I sat down, shellshocked. She said she had more pictures somewhere, and that she'd try to dig them out. And she was as good as her word, bless her. A few days later an email arrived, packed with dates and facts, and a load more photos.

Of course, I have thanked her profusely. But you know, it's a funny thing. She seems just as grateful. Just as it delights me to be handed a 1957 photo of my house, my new friend seems every bit as thrilled that I care. There's an unspoken mutual connection. As custodians of this rough old pile of stones and cob, we've both engaged with a tiny part of Cornish history, and it's quite a special feeling.

Gardener

2017

I n my previous life in the London publishing world, I had the privilege of working with the *Royal Horticultural Society* on several of their huge and impressive books. It was an inspirational experience working with some of the top plant experts in the world (the free press pass to the *Chelsea Flower Show* every spring was a bonus), and it ignited a passion for plants that burns on, over twenty years later.

As a result, when I returned to Cornwall at the beginning of the century, I was keen to step things up a notch. I enrolled in a horticulture course at Duchy College, and made lots of new gardening friends, a number of whom were professional gardeners. I even took on looking after a few people's gardens myself. But something obvious soon struck me: what a wide-ranging set of skills the professional gardener needs to have, and yet how frequently these skills go underappreciated. I wondered why. Are a gardener's talents compromised somewhat by the fact that we are all, to some extent, *gardeners*? You'll probably call yourself a gardener even if all you ever do is water a window box once a month. You can't really say the same about solicitors – it's not as if you'd have a go at a bit of corporate law a couple of times a year, the same way you'd have a stab at pruning your privet.

And I suppose it's true that many of the more mundane gardening jobs are very easy. Things you could practically train a monkey to do: mow the lawn, rake leaves, turn a compost heap, that kind of thing. Basic 'maintenance gardening'. Ah, but ask that same monkey to decide, on the spot, which pruning group your hybrid tea rose falls into, or whether that's powdery or downy mildew on your grapevine, or which out of a bed full of annual 'weeds' are not weeds at all, but desirable seedlings, and more than likely that monkey's going to disgrace itself.

OK, enough monkey metaphors. The point is, a good gardener has a unique and wide-ranging set of skills too numerous to list, but which include plant identification, manual dexterity, ability to plan, knowledge of pests and diseases, creativity and physical fitness. Sure, there are cowboys out there, but a good gardener is truly multi-skilled, and such skills are not learned overnight – they come from years of experience and dedication. And yet they're just a gardener. It's a noble profession, yes, but so frequently undervalued.

Perhaps when you opt for a life with dirt under your fingernails, there will always be people who will dismiss you as someone with, well, dirt under your fingernails. One of my grandfathers made his living as a gardener all his life (the war years notwithstanding), first at Trewithen, then Penair, then at Chiverton, working for Treve Holman. He was evidently held in high regard, indeed at one point he was approached by the Foxes at Glendurgan, no less (I remember my mother telling me about how she and the whole family were invited to tea there to meet the family). My grandfather was offered the job as a result, but opted to stay at Penair. So as gardeners go, he had a reasonably high status. Yet his pay was low, and the Cornish rural life in which my mother describes growing up was a long way from the bucolic idyll – it was nothing short of poverty. Until the day he died, my grandfather never dreamed of owning a car, or a telephone, or any kind of heating other than a single log fire. He never expected to. He was just a gardener.

So I think it would be nice if we re-evaluated our professional gardeners. And next time we spot one at work, remember there's probably an awful lot more to them than meets the eye.

Even if they do happen to be raking leaves at the time.

Clearing your head

2010

I was on the beach the other day, staring at the sea. Suddenly I realised ten minutes had gone by. In that time, my mind had raced through subjects as diverse as the looming 2012 Olympics, what the twins were having for tea, Christmas, whether I regret selling my motorcycle so much that I should consider getting another one (despite the undeniable accident statistics and the fact that I now have parental responsibility), Ed Miliband, cuttlefish, and shoes.

And it made me think. If you take a quick glimpse at the sea, you just see the sea. If you watch it for longer, things start to happen. Not only do you start to notice more (its condition, the wind, the smell, the birds, the sky, the light...), but your head soon gets onto another level altogether. Hence the Ed Miliband/cuttlefish thing.

Now I'm no psychiatrist, but it seems to me that it's only when you de-clutter your head that your brain can really let rip like this. In my pretentious art student days, I was into abstract expressionism. I remember reading a quote by the American painter Barnett Newman, in which he stated: "Rather than working with fragments of space, I now work with space as a totality". Not only does this sound great, but it's the perfect excuse to produce vast canvasses of nothingness. That's what

Newman did with his *colour field* paintings in the 1950s: just a whopping void of yellow, with a slim, slightly darker yellow stripe along the bottom. Or a big mass of flat red, with a slightly different coloured line going up each side. Of course, 99% of people think this sort of art is, at best, overrated rubbish, and at worst, *fraudulent* rubbish. But I defy anyone to sit in a gallery and look at a real Barnett Newman, or Rothko, or Jackson Pollock, and not get something quite surprising from the experience. Even if it's just to clear your head and be transported to another place.

That's what people often don't understand about abstract art – that there is no official required response: it's *up to you*. It really doesn't matter if you love it or hate it, but at least have a look at it and see what happens. Staring at the sea is very similar, except that we're not overburdened with a self-perceived obligation to respond to it in an appropriate way (we haven't paid to get into the gallery to see it, which helps).

But the sea/art comparison goes beyond abstract painting. Great art, in all its manifestations, is often presented in a surprisingly uncomplicated package. There are so many famous examples of artistic endeavour which are deceptively simple. Think of *Waiting for Godot*; a play in which two tramps wait for somebody by a tree, but widely regarded as one of the 20th century's greatest plays. Or Orwell's *Animal Farm*. Or a Barbara Hepworth sculpture. Or the *Angel of the North*. Or *Jonathan Livingston Seagull*. They can all reveal as many layers as you want. You just need to give them a bit of time (of course it doesn't always work. I read the much-lauded 'allegorical

143

fable' *The Alchemist* by Paulo Coelho and it just left me confused and resentful).

The problem is that sometimes you can take this theory to extremes. If you stare at anything for long enough, in the hope that you will find some sort of personal truth, your mind can start going to some very strange places. It happened to me with *Peppa Pig*. I started out dismissing it as a rather two dimensional, simplistically drawn children's TV show. But after a few months I'd convinced myself that it was dealing with some complex issues of sibling rivalry, the importance of paternal responsibility, and, quite possibly, a metaphor for the collapse of Empire.

Maybe I went a bit far with *Peppa Pig*. But I do think it's a lot more interesting than *The Alchemist*.

Starling

2012

F or the past thirteen years, I've kept a list of bird species
seen in my garden. No, hang on a minute, don't go. I'm
no twitcher, honestly, and this list isn't one of those obsessive,
nerdy things. Like a lot of people, I admit that I do like birds,
and that I do find it fascinating to build a picture of exactly
what has, at some point in its life, considered my humble bit of
the planet worthy of a visit. A little light data-collecting,
nothing more.

The current tally is 35 species. Thirty-five types of bird have
been tempted by what I have to offer (oh yes, I have bird
feeders, and plenty of 'em. And nestboxes, and birdbaths). 35 is
a total I'm quite proud of, and I'm not convinced it shouldn't
be even more, especially when you consider that if a siskin
landed on one of my feeders I'd probably dismiss it as a funny
looking greenfinch. Plus, I'm sure I've seen the odd little
brown warblery-thing in the bushes out the back from time to
time, and I'm fairly convinced it was either a willow warbler or
a garden warbler. Or maybe a chiffchaff. But with no exact
identification, I haven't counted it. So actually the real total
might be nearer forty.

Some highlights do stand out in my mind from over the
years. There was the fully-grown buzzard that took to perching

on the back of a chair in the front garden not twenty feet from the kitchen door, persisting as if it had something to tell me. Or the barn owl we often see on summer evenings, perched atop the telegraph pole (which is planted firmly within the boundary of my garden, so yes, it counts). Then there are the regular visits from frantic flocks of long tailed tits, the now daily visits from our resident woodpeckers, the stunning bullfinches, the winter blackcaps and fieldfares...

But there's one surprising absentee. A bird that, according to the 2012 *RSPB Big Garden Birdwatch*, is the 2nd commonest garden bird in Britain. Honestly, if 35 other types of bird have had cause to be seduced by the patch of earth surrounding my house, you'd think the common or garden starling might have had the decency to put in an occasional appearance.

It's a seriously ubiquitous bird, the starling. It's equally at home scavenging on city pavements as it is foraging in remote rural fields, or picking its way through seaweed on the shoreline, come to that. Paradoxically it's a bird often dismissed as dull and scruffy and yet, with the light on it, has plumage as iridescently stunning as anything you'll ever see attached to a bird.

But an even bigger paradox with this overlooked little chap is that it's responsible for one of the most amazing wildlife spectacles you'll ever see: the famous winter starling roost. We have our own Cornish one down at Marazion, where, if you time it right, you'll see a huge flock of thousands forming wave upon wave of almost incomprehensible, pulsating black ribbons in the sky.

146

One starling, that's all I ask. But yet they remain, *out there somewhere*, too busy to fit me in. That's nature for you. The fact is, my garden is right on the edge of a coastal scrub landscape. Within a few hundred yards of here I've seen wheatears, meadow pipits, skylarks and stonechats. But they don't need me either. They know what they need, and they stay put. I suppose starlings are no different. Blue tits come into our gardens all the time, because they've happily adapted, and redwings do so a bit more reluctantly, when it suits them in winter. But with some species it's just never going to happen. I suppose it's a good sign really, that there are still some birds that haven't had to resort to creeping into our gardens in search of food.

I'm just going to have to learn to live with it.

That scything scene

2015

O h come on, let's talk about *Poldark* again. You know you want to. Filming for series two is underway, and in the meantime series one has been lapped up in America, so like many people, I've recently found myself re-watching the first series. A few more things have struck me, which I'd like to share with the group.

Firstly, *that* scything scene. Ross attacked that hay like a man possessed. Much has been made of Aidan Turner's frantic, incompetent technique. It's true – I have a friend who does a lot of scything, and he gets the job done with a delightfully slow and easy motion. But wait a minute – let's not be too hasty. Ross had just seen his friend Jim sentenced to two years in jail (and, effectively, death). He was hopping mad, and his scything suffered. He was seething, and he took it out on his scything (of course, Ross's seething scything notwithstanding, we're all well aware that this was the director's best opportunity to show off Aidan's sweaty gym abs. And those abs get bums on seats).

No, I'm more troubled by Ross's perma-stubble. He must shave at least every couple of days, because he's always got a day or two's worth of beard. But I'm fairly confident that rufty tufty eighteenth century mercenary types like him would have been unacquainted with the grooming products so familiar to today's metrosexual male. So why is he never seen clean-shaven? You'd think he might have had a wash and brush up for the posh ball in Truro but no, he rocks up as always, all stubbly, looking like he's been dragged through a very sexy hedge backwards.

This will probably, one day, date this production, just as the 1975-77 version now looks 'of its time' due to, among several other things, Robin Ellis's plausibly-eighteenth-century-yet-incongruously-seventies-looking hair. In another forty years' time when they remake it again (and they probably will), I'm fairly certain that Ross won't have designer stubble and a well-oiled bob.

Another disconcerting thing: No matter how much of a hurry our eponymous hero is in to get from Nampara to Trenwith, or fro Truro to home, why does he always choose a route that is, by definition, extremely circuitous? You don't take the coast path if you're in a hurry Ross! Or when travelling *inland*! Of course it all looks fantastic, and *Visit Cornwall* (or whatever they're called now) must have been licking their lips, but I tell you, it ent right.

OK, just one more observation for now: There's a small snag with casting such a young and gorgeous actor as Ross Poldark: Ross is 23 at the beginning of the first book. If they continue to make one TV series covering two books per year, then in 5 years' time as book 12 draws to a close, Aidan Turner will be playing Ross pushing sixty. Aidan Turner isn't going to look like a man pushing sixty anytime soon. Maybe they could phase Robin Ellis back in. Except they've gone and made him evil Reverend Halse.

It seems an eternity ago that we were agonizing over whether the new *Poldark* would measure up against the books/original series. A mere eighteen months ago, the founder of the *Poldark* Appreciation Society was quoted saying of the recently cast Aidan Turner "...a more masculine actor would have stood a better chance. A lamb to the slaughter comes to mind". I'm quite sure Mr Turner didn't lose too much sleep over such a misguided comment then, and the only thing worrying him now is probably whether to become the next James Bond or just settle for life as an ordinary Hollywood A-lister. The fact is that this *Poldark* rebirth is brilliant, and, in my opinion, more true to the books than the first TV adaptation (which I loved) ever was. There will always be a handful of pedants freeze-framing a scene to point at a distant burglar alarm and scoff, but the fact is, practically all of us have been won over.

Which brings me to my biggest concern: how on earth are we going to get through the next six months waiting for series two?

Gasometer

2015

They've just been talking about gasometers on the radio. These vast cylinders have been part of the British urban landscape for 200 years, apparently. No longer considered necessary, they've been disappearing over the past twenty-odd years, and now the final few hundred are being sold off, creating extremely lucrative development sites. Seems reasonable – we simply don't need them any more.

Design guru Stephen Bayley, who's always got something interesting to say, is a massive fan of the gasometer. Evangelical he was, calling them 'an almost perfect reconciliation of form and function and purpose and style'. He'd rather they didn't get dismantled at all, implying that gasometers could be in some way be given a new lease of life, while still retaining their integral beauty. 'Creative re-use' is the buzzword. Bayley even sees them as art.

Now hang on a minute, I thought. Art? Gasometers? There's an obvious link here. Wasn't Cornwall's most famous gasometer, the one on the seafront in St Ives, replaced in 1993 by, of all things, an art gallery? And not any old art gallery, but a branch of the Tate, no less.

Now I've always rather liked gasometers too – despite the fact that they're basically a huge, industrial storage tank, there is something spectacular about them. In the right light, obviously. But I wouldn't want to go using trendy words like 're-purpose' or 'creative re-use'. I'm all for 're-purposing' an old crate you might find on the beach as a rustic, driftwood-style set of shelves, but my wizened brain struggles to imagine how you'd efficiently reconfigure a vast great gas holder as something useful. Let alone that ugly, rusty thing I remember in St Ives.

I expect the Tate architects would probably argue that they've paid due respect to the original gasometer with their huge, disappointingly viewless and consequently deserted, gasometer-shaped entrance hall. As you've probably surmised, I've never been a fan of the Tate building – I clearly recall, as an art graduate myself, my first excited visit to the 'Tate of the West' as it was known then. As I wandered through the cavernous halls, staircases and mezzanines I started to wonder if I was ever going to clap eyes on anything I'd come to see (Patrick Heron's colourful window notwithstanding). It seemed a bizarre waste of space. A massive, classy, architectural showpiece, yes, but in a town so agonizingly short of room! Surprise surprise, within a few years they started talking about having to extend it, blaming increased visitor numbers.

Anyway, enough of my personal misgivings. I'm confident that even if others agree with me about the Tate building, this wouldn't make the original rusty old gasometer a preferable thing to look at. But it does make you marvel to think there was ever a time when plonking a gasometer in such a stunning location was considered an appropriate thing to do. The fact is, when the gasometer was erected in St Ives all those years ago, I'm quite sure no-one batted an eyelid. In that road, back then, there were fisherman's cottages, net lofts, a gasometer, and a graveyard. All necessary, functional things. Then came the artists' studios, the galleries, and the holiday flats. These days, parking spaces are selling for fifty grand each. How times change.

Something similar's about to happen to Britain's most famous gasometer – the one at the Oval cricket ground (as in 'Warne's coming in to bowl from the gasometer end'). In a few years' time, Londoners will probably stand and gaze upon the billions of pounds' worth of fabulous flats which fill the Oval gasometer site, and struggle to recollect that there was ever such a structure there, that something so vast and obsolete could have hung on for so long. Just as I now find myself standing in St Ives, trying to remember a thing like that where the Tate now stands, on the seafront in a town so desirable that fishermen's cottages now sell for a quarter of a million pounds.

The fact that a gasometer was ever there is a reminder of how a place can transform itself. In Cornwall, or anywhere.

* The following year, the Oval's Victorian gasometer was given Grade II listed status and protected from demolition.

Social media

2010

W hen I was a teenager in the seventies, we had some pretty strange ideas about 'The Future'. There was a feeling that it was going to start arriving very fast, but we weren't really sure just how. Certainly I remember thinking that by the turn of the century we'd be eating roast beef flavoured paste from a tube, like the astronauts did, and that that would be preferable to eating real roast beef. We really did think that. But then we also thought that Cadbury's Smash tasted better than mashed potato. And of course we all assumed that we'd be holidaying on the moon in the impossibly futuristic-sounding *Year 2000*. Looking back, it was a world of deluded, blissful ignorance.

There was one thing we got right though. We thought computers would take over the world by now, and they pretty much have. But strangely, computers are now not the sole preserve of that kid who sat in the front of class, wore glasses and actually enjoyed maths. Computers are considered OK now. There's no stigma. They are cool. I really wasn't expecting this.

There's no better example of this phenomenon than my cousin Olly. Olly was born twenty years after me. He works for a big computer company, doing something I can only guess at.

Last time I asked him, he said something like, "*I'm working with an upgraded ST22 app providing functionality to deploy fault-tolerant, distributed, multi-tier Bongo software, based largely on modular components running on a high end server.*" He's quite oblivious to how this sounds to people like me. I react to hearing this sort of sentence the same way I react to hearing techno music. It makes me, well, tense. It sits entirely outside of my own world of experience or understanding. It gives me an almost uncontrollable urge to go camping in the woods. But I'm entirely aware that it's people who are comfortable with this sort of sentence who are running the world these days.

Here's the thing though. Olly isn't a pasty-faced square-eyed geek. He surfs. He's got a shiny, souped-up van, and has good taste in music. You'd like him.

Olly's got his finger on the pulse. Lots of pulses. And Olly's put me straight on a thing or two. He says I have to up my profile. Olly says I've been writing this column for years, and yet I've got no idea who's reading it. Not strictly true, as I get comments, and interesting emails. Sometimes. But Olly says I need to do more. A blog, or *Facebook,* or *Twitter,* or something. I've always assumed that the reason people like me don't get involved with this sort of thing is because we all have lives. Better things to do than all this self-indulgent, meaningless titillation so beloved of self-obsessed teenage narcissists. But Olly says it's not like that – it can open doors, and introduce you to fascinating new people, and there's a community out there who aren't necessarily housebound, lifeless computer nerds. So I looked at *Facebook,* and there were indeed a lot of pictures of people looking cool, wearing sunglasses, being wacky at parties, on the beach, that kind of thing.

So I'm going to enter the second decade of the millennium by moving with the times. I'm going to grab the zeitgeist, and pretend that I like it. Knowing my luck, someone will now announce that the blog is dead, and that suddenly it's cool to keep yourself to yourself. Surely deep down we all know that that would be absolutely lovely, don't we?

So, I now have a page on *Facebook*. The idea, says Olly, is that you look at it, and comment. So please, if you have the slightest idea about this sort of thing, go onto my *Facebook Backalong* page and say something. I have absolutely no idea if anyone out there is remotely interested in this, but maybe, just maybe, this could be the start of something vaguely meaningful. We are, after all, a tenth of the way through the first century of the third millennium.

* Sorry Olly. Years have passed, and I still have virtually no idea what I'm supposed to be doing on Facebook.

Cold

2009

L ast month I listed my top ten favourite things about Cornwall, so this month I was considering writing my top ten least favourite things. But then I thought this upbeat, aspirational sort of a magazine really isn't the place for such negativity. And anyway I couldn't come up with ten things. Six maybe. Or seven, if you count what I want to complain about this month.

Last winter, if you recall, Cornwall rather let us down. This subtropical paradise we call home turned into something unrecognisable. We had snow. The real thing, not like the usual Cornish stuff which falls once every seven years, turns to sleet after 45 seconds, completely vanishes in the time it takes to say, "Mother, where's me mittens?" and leaves us all feeling a bit, well, cheated.

Last January, there must have been a good three or four inches of it. That's the inconvenience equivalent of about six feet to a Canadian. But I didn't mind the snow, apart from the annoying timing that it was the boys' first winter and because they were only one-year-old, they just sort of looked at as if to say "Hmm, the world's a bit of a funny colour today". What a wasted opportunity, because chances are they'll never look upon such a deluge again for the rest of their childhood.

No, it was the far colder weather we had a month or so before the snowfall that got to me. In some places it hit double figures, *below freezing*. In Cornwall! You know, like it does in proper cold countries, where people ski and things. It was terrifying. Most annoying of all was that I'd been spouting on in this very column about how privileged we are to be able to grow tender exotica in our gardens here without ever worrying about it. In particular, I was talking about echiums, those massive spikes of blue flowers gracing gardens and hedgerows all over Cornwall every summer. And as the magazine went to press, I found myself gazing out of the window at dozens of vertical, black, previously echium-shaped shrivelled sticks, once so full of promise, all having succumbed to the completely unexpected and distinctly un-Cornish temperatures. 'I'm going to look like an idiot. Again,' I thought.

An echium is only hardy down to about minus five degrees centigrade. And minus five degrees centigrade would have been a pretty balmy day in early January 2009, such was its Arctic ferocity. So what chance did these plants from the Canary Isles have? It goes without saying that many other garden exotics were also gonners: aeoniums, echevarias... But it was worse than that. Plants that I'd assumed were reasonably tough had also bitten the dust. I lost two salvias, a correa, numerous osteospermums...

With all the talk of global warming, I think we've rather been lulled into a false sense of security, horticulturally speaking. But even though we'd got used to the seasons here merging into a sustained period of mild drizzle during which time it rarely drops anywhere near freezing, last winter we had, what you might call, *a bit of weather*. Of course, more experienced gardeners than me know that this happens every once in a while. One such person reminded me that osteospermums used to be grown as an annual, and thrown away at the end of the season. We didn't used to be so presumptuous as to think they'd stay alive year after year. And now I've learned it the hard way.

Well, I'm not going to make the same mistake again. What was I thinking? You can forget all those daft plants from sunny climes. You can keep your palm trees. I'm over it. I won't be caught out like that again. I'm thinking cabbages. Not the poncy ornamental ones, neither. The normal ones, like you're supposed to grow in Cornwall. They're perfectly attractive if you squint. And hold your nose.

Flip-flop

2016

A funny thing happened recently. Picture the scene: it's a hot, late summer's day, and the whole family return from an afternoon on the beach. I rinse all the wetsuits out, and everyone's shoes, of course, lest they reek of rancid fish food in that way they do when they've been in the sea then left to dry. This included my favourite flip-flops.

They're the best ones I've ever owned. Posh ones. Not posh enough to call a sandal, but made of robust, sun-bleached fabric, pleasantly weathered, with soles now nicely compacted to the point where they caress my weird arches like two bespoke, mini memory-foam mattresses. Every time I put them on, they give me that familiar reassurance you only get from an old friend.

The weather was set fair, and after a good rinse I left the flip-flops on the front lawn overnight, as I had a hundred times before, so that the next day's early morning sun would dry them out in time for me to pop them straight on, all dry and lovely, in the morning. And guess what. Next morning, only one was there. Exactly where I'd left it, but very much alone. I couldn't believe my eyes. I just stood there and stared, reflecting on how 50% of a pair of shoes is worth considerably less than 50% of a pair of shoes.

My first thought was badgers. They've always been regular visitors during the night – you can tell from the diggings all over the lawn. Or foxes, I suppose – there are plenty of those about too. Yes, I can just imagine a young fox excitedly grabbing a nice spongy flip-flop for a bit of chewing practice, then jettisoning it in some dark hedgerow down the road somewhere. Or it could even have been a rook. I've seen them pick up detritus bigger than cricket stumps at nesting time. In fact some years ago, my next-door neighbours Paul and Felicity kept finding golf balls in their field. They were well into double figures when they noticed that one of the balls had the name of the local driving range on it. They dutifully returned seventeen balls to the driving range people, who explained that it had been going on for months. Presumably the pesky birds mistook them for eggs, although why exactly they kept flying five miles then dropping them in the same spot, no-one knows.

Then there was the time my wife lost the watch she used to wear for work. Years later, I spotted it nestled in the grass at the end of our back paddock, its rubber strap nibbled to stumps by rabbits. After much head-scratching, we concluded that it must have dropped from the pocket of her nurse's uniform which had been hanging on the line to dry. The point is, strange things happen. I can only guess at what nocturnal shenanigans brought about the disappearance of my cherished shoe.

Anyway, I began the search. I even bribed my boys to help. But it felt hopeless from the start. The lost flip-flop could have been absolutely anywhere. I don't know which was more tedious – searching among the bindweed-choked shrubs of every nearby border in a forlorn attempt to spot that faded, frustratingly leaf-coloured shoe, or putting up with everyone hilariously telling me they'd keep an eye out for any shifty-looking, one-legged people wearing a size nine, green flip-flop.

I'm coming to terms with the fact that it's probably gone for good. But I haven't chucked out the remaining flip-flop, just in case. You never know. In the meantime, thanks for bearing with me in what is admittedly a frivolous subject this month, but I just wanted to put it out there. If anyone's experienced anything similar, please get in touch. Someone may have a useful tip. I have a strong feeling that it's still languishing under a hedge somewhere. Even if it's unwearable, it would be a relief to solve the mystery. I need closure. In the meantime I've bought new flip-flops. But they're rubbish. I dislike them about as much as I loved my old ones.

I mean, they don't even make the right noise.

Furzey bush

2017

For years, I've been half-heartedly trying to remove a straggly old furzey bush from a bank in my back garden. It's not that I don't like it – it's just in the wrong place. Every time I think I've successfully ended its life, it comes right back at me, its resolve stiffened. Worse, little versions of it start sprouting up all around it. In short, I think I've failed.

Humble gorse is, of course, a bit of a brute. More often than not, it's bad news for other plants trying to survive in its company. Someone thought it a jolly good idea to plant our European gorse as hedging in New Zealand many years ago, and now it's an invasive and persistent weed, putting paid to countless native species, and enjoying about the same popularity there as the millions of American grey squirrels that have spread all over the UK.

Gorse is everywhere here in Cornwall, largely due to its ability to survive where other plants fear to tread (the poorest of soil or mine waste). Its oiliness, combined with its tendency to hang onto dry, dead branches, make it highly flammable. So a carelessly jettisoned cigarette butt (or, in the case of a roadside hill near me, a spark from the annual parade of traction engines) can put paid to large areas of vegetation. But even when burnt to a frazzle, the tenacious gorse comes right back at you – its charred remains regenerating like the Terminator, again to the detriment of other plants that weren't so lucky. It's a sprawling, vicious, spiky, invasive beast of a plant, is gorse.

Hmm. And yet. What's the single most *Cornish* sight you can think of? A majestic chough, perhaps, soaring across an azure blue sky? A lone fishing boat, chugging out of a picturesque harbour at dawn? No? OK, what about a scarlet holidaymaker wiping dog poo off the bottom of their Crocs on the coast path? Gull picking chips out of a bin?

For me, the most quintessentially Cornish sight has to be a perky stonechat, perched atop a flowering gorse bush, nestling among purple heather, on a cliff top. That, truly, is a stunning sight – so many elements rolled into one. Ten minutes' walk from my front door, these plants turn what could be a bleak landscape of gravelly mine waste into something wondrous. There's nothing more Cornish. And it wouldn't be the same without our omnipresent gorse bushes.

But their significance in Cornwall goes far beyond mere aesthetics – for centuries, the plant has been culturally useful. My mother clearly remembers collecting gorse for fuel while living with her grandmother in Summercourt during World War Two. Every Monday was wash day, and the big hot water vessel they called a 'copper' had to be heated pronto if they were to get the job done in a day. After fetching water from the well, it was the kids' job to go out onto Goss Moor and collect the furze. It was horrible, black, spiky, sooty stuff, having already been burned on the moor, but the young children would carefully tie it up in bundles and stagger back to the house with it.

Gorse also does a great job stabilizing poor soil. In many locations it's a very effective windbreak, or even hedging, if you don't mind it on the 'informal' side. And there's nothing like that amazing coconutty scent (OK, maybe a coconut). It's a delightful thing when it hits you on a hot day when walking the coast path. Gorse is great for wildlife: birds and insects love it. And, being from the legume family, it fixes nitrogen in the soil, actually improving it for other plants.

Quite a list. Maybe this often-maligned plant isn't so bad after all. There's definitely more to it than meets the eye. So I think I'm going to step it up a notch. Think outside the box. I'm going to go out in the back garden and pick some beautiful, fragrant gorse stems to put in a vase.

Now, where did I leave my leather welding gauntlets...

Fifty-three

2015

I just turned fifty-three. What a rubbish number. Such a long time to wait 'til the next big milestone when there's an excuse to have a party, but enough time having elapsed since I turned a youthful, spritely fifty to regret that I was too depressed to have a big do. How can I be fifty-three? I've got a skateboard!

Soon I'll catch myself doing what all old people do: exaggerating how old they are. You hear them most days on the lunchtime phone-in. When asked their age, they never say 'I'm seventy-eight', but always the rather more convoluted 'I'll be seventy-nine in June!' The other day I honestly heard a lady say 'In April, I'll be seventy-three and a half!' What is this about? I want no part of it!

What's more, I'm sure that various events are conspiring to rub my nose in the fact that I'm approaching my dotage. Things that remind me that the world was a better place yesteryear (good grief, who even uses words like '*yesteryear*' anyway? Old people, that's who). For example, every time I walk down a high street I'm aware of an unfathomable new trend: old tat is apparently now stylish and desirable. You see shops full of this stuff that you couldn't have given away five years ago. Wobbly looking teak furniture from the seventies.

Orange and brown soft furnishings. Vile, mass produced floral ceramics. Any old rubbish preceded by the word 'vintage' or 'retro'. I suppose when a new generation comes along who don't quite remember something, they develop a hankering for it, and it gets trendy again. Look at cider. And beards.

And then there's Truro police station. Few things remind you of your advancing decrepitude like the sad demise of something you remember as bright and new. About a year ago, I watched aghast as they flattened a building that I clearly recall being built in 1969. Everyone was talking about it back then. The new police station was *really* modern – all exposed corridors and cubes and glass – huge, grey and austere. It stood out like a sore thumb, galvanizing opinion, as these things always do, into either a) 'hideous, modernist carbuncle' (the vast majority) or b) 'brave, brutalist statement'. Years later, it was even considered by some to be sufficiently significant to be worthy of listing. Well, it was certainly 'listing' when the developers reduced the whole senile building to rubble in order to redevelop the site as flats. I stood there watching for a bit. And it made my own impending infirmity seem all the more real.

There are plenty of other things reminding me of my imminent frailty. My contemporaries who had their children at an appropriate age (unlike me) are becoming grandparents. The doctor's told me that I've officially got arthritis in my shoulder (and, I suspect, numerous other places I'm too scared to mention to him). It's horrible. A friend I've known since we were both a year old recently grew a beard of such magnitude and whiteness that he looks like a cross between Santa Claus and Uncle Albert from *Only Fools and Horses*. It really suits him. We are the same age. Oh, and I read recently that the average Briton on holiday takes over 400 photos. *Four hundred*. That's more than ten rolls of 36 exposure film (you remember: *film*. Yes, from the *olden days*). And apparently 45 of these are 'selfies'. I will never do this, and will never understand those who do. I am, therefore, out of step with modern life.

I've decided that I'm not going to give in though. I'm making a New Year's resolution to fight this wretched, inevitable decline. The *Saga* brochures that have been flying, unopened, directly from doormat to recycling bin can just keep on (then again, there is a small part of me that actually does quite fancy a nice coach tour of the Cotswolds. Hey, I could take my skateboard!).

In the meantime, here's wishing you a very Happy Christmas. I'm off for a little lie down. After all I'll be fifty-four next birthday.

Quoit

2016

We went for a walk recently, the missus and me. One of the last mighty storms of winter was finally starting to abate, we'd put the time aside, so out we strode along the drenched lanes around Pendarves Woods near Camborne.

It was great. The clouds cleared, allowing us a delicious, much-needed glimpse of weak sun, and we unexpectedly stumbled upon a lovely thing. There, in the middle of a field, was a beautiful quoit. It was so dramatically situated, so statuesque, so *obvious*, that we couldn't work out why it had previously eluded us. I've visited plenty of ancient Cornish sites over the years: Lanyon, Chun, Merry Maidens, Men-an-Tol…certainly all the obvious ones. They're everywhere, after all. We've got friends who have a significant Bronze Age *fogou* on their farm in West Penwith for goodness sake. But this particular quoit is quite close to where we live, and yet we'd never seen it, until this particular day. There it stood, proud and immaculate, casting long shadows across the landscape. Perfect. Too perfect, almost.

Then we read the helpful interpretive signage, and all became clear. No wonder it looked so new. Last time we walked this way we'd have gone right past it, because a few years ago *Carwynnen Quoit* was nothing more than a scruffy pile of granite. Thanks to a dedicated team of professionals, volunteers and some significant funding, the collapsed landmark had been restored to its former glory in 2014. How fantastic.

Except that part of me felt a little let down. I mean, they'd used cranes, and 21st century technology, and I had this niggling feeling that this made the whole thing a bit, well, *bogus*. The knowledge that all this was achieved by people in high-vis tabards, and hard hats, with clipboards, and machinery, and inspections, and risk assessments, seemed *non-authentic*. I wanted it to have been done in period costume, with rollers, and levers, and lots of grunting. And the fact that it now looked so tidy seemed to somehow undermine its historical credibility.

Which is, of course, ridiculous. This quoit is 5,000 years old. *Five thousand years*. That's longer than I've been writing this column! Sure, *Carwynnen Quoit* probably didn't look exactly like this when it was built as a burial monument sometime around 3,000 BC. But then the entire landscape would have been unrecognisable anyway. This quoit has been victim to the ravages of time for millennia. I don't suppose anyone really knows exactly how the site changed for its first few thousand years, but it's well documented that it collapsed in the mid nineteenth century, was re-erected, then collapsed again in the mid 1960s. That's just the last 150 years. It's been given a new lease of life, and that's what matters.

Around the same time, I'd just been hearing about the new carving in the rocks at Tintagel. There was hell up because

English(!) *Heritage* had seen fit to carve an approximation of Merlin's face into the virgin rocks on the beach below the castle, like Mount Rushmore. Now, as an example of art in the landscape, it's certainly nothing to get excited about. And it's not nearly as nice as, say, that lovely grassy recumbent lady lying by the path at Heligan, which is indulgent, and striking, and unexpected, and doesn't pretend to be much more. This Merlin face is a tacky stunt to drag in a few extra paying punters, and it could be said that accusations of insensitivity at a sacred site are justified. However, unlike Mount Rushmore, it's weeny – hardly any bigger than an actual face. A bit of fun for the kiddies to hunt for, like the Mermaid of Zennor carved into the pew at Zennor Church. Sure, both may be a bit of an anti-climax when you find them, but it's not about the destination, it's about the search.

I can live with a disappointingly immaculate quoit, and if a seven-year-old's search for 'Merlin's actual face' in the rocks ignites a spark of interest in history, I'd say that vandalising a small bit of rock is justifiable too.

Challenge

2016

I've been trying to assemble some coherent thoughts about the whole Brexit thing, so that I might share them with you. But as I type, whatever point I was trying to make becomes submerged in a quagmire of expletives, and I end up googling house prices in Canada. You deserve better than that. So at least for this month I'll avoid the subject on this page, take a deep breath, count to ten, and talk about something a little more, well, *light*. Again.

Actually before I do that, I'd like to just take this opportunity to express my gratitude to a member of the *Cornwall Today* team whose work may, I suspect, sometimes go unappreciated. I'm talking about this magazine's designer, Ed. I'm very aware that without his creative skills, my turgid prose would have withered on this page long ago. It is he who visually embellishes my dry waffle every month, enhancing it with an appropriate illustration or motif just enough to entice the reluctant reader into giving the first paragraph a go, the vain hope being that they might then be dragged kicking and screaming all the way to the end of this monthly seven hundred words.

Situated here on the back page, this column is theoretically the issue's last hurrah before the reader closes its glossy pages and adds it to the dusty magazine pile next to the upstairs loo, under the little dish of potpourri you put there last Christmas which is now mostly dead woodlice and fluff but you'd rather not touch because it's, well, next to the toilet. Or alternatively you pop it into the bag of mags destined for the doctor's waiting room. Or dentist's. Or hairdresser's. I'm not saying that's necessarily where this fine organ deserves to end up. I'm just saying that these places are where all magazines, inevitably, *do*. That's one thing you can say about *Cornwall Today* – no matter how deeply you digest its content, like a fine meal, you just never know when it's going to jump up and repeat on you. In the nicest possible way.

Anyway, back to Ed the design guy. He's plainly a chap who possesses two oft-incompatible skills: creativity, and technical knowhow. Although I've always been appreciative of what he's done for this column over the years, I probably wouldn't have mentioned it on this page, were it not for the fact that recently he's upped his game noticeably. For example, a few months ago I wrote about the new carving of Merlin on the rocks at Tintagel. Now Ed didn't just type 'wizard' into some online photo library and slap the pic down onto a backdrop of a beach. Oh no, the creative juices were flowing that day. When I opened the back page I was stunned to see myself convincingly transformed into a pointy-hatted wizard with a flowing beard so long and dense and realistic that I was almost taken in by it myself. I found myself longingly caressing my cheeks and fantasizing about how it would feel to cultivate such a magnificent and lustrous thing. It was hilarious. It provoked comments. But there was more. In last month's edition he stepped it up a notch again, magicking up a convincing tableau involving me driving a van, complete with smiling, surrogate family.

I'm not sure what's happening, but it seems whatever challenge I set him, Ed's rising to it. It's got to the point now where every month, I open *Cornwall Today* with a mounting sense of anticipation, keen to see what on earth has emerged from his creative mind and taken form here on the back page.

But I digress. Back to this month's subject: my forthcoming gender readjustment programme, how it might impact on my place in the queue as a space tourist for the 2033 Mars trip, and who's going to look after my flock of pedigree longhorn cattle while I'm away.

Oh no, hang on, I'm out of space.

Sluggish

2015

I'm very fond of my garden here on the north coast. It's big – the best part of an acre – and fairly well packed with plants. All the usual Cornish suspects are here: cordyline palms, plenty of hedging fuchsias, bulletproof eleagnus, hebes and phormiums, clumps of agapanthus looking lovely in summer, Michaelmas daisies in autumn, the obligatory fatsia japonica, and as many echiums as I can manage, depending how brutal the previous winter's been.

You get the idea. But there's a problem, a problem revealed by which plants are absent. There are no hostas, nor lupins. Neither are there any cannas or delphiniums. I love them, and I've tried growing them all over the past sixteen years. But I've failed miserably.

Slugs and snails have fought such a sustained campaign against me that I'm thinking of throwing in the towel. I fought on gamely for years, testing most of the recommended slug/snail deterrents: beer traps, salt, nematodes. They all worked, a bit, for a while. I even tried Monty Don's laborious, nightly, manual slug-removal-by-torchlight system. The latter being do-able for a pocket handkerchief townie garden, but necessitating hours of fruitless labour in a whopping rural one. It seems that if you remove a couple of hundred slugs one rainy night, their vile cohorts will be lining up to replace them the next.

Then I read somewhere that the average-sized British garden contains 20,000 slugs. *Twenty thousand*. At this point I pretty much lost the will to fight. I realised just how unfairly the cards were stacked against me. I still do what I can to combat the problem, within reasonable parameters. These days I only plant seedlings out when they're big and tough enough for slugs and snails to turn their slimy little noses up at them. I still refuse to use slug pellets, as I'd hate to poison a bird. But I let the chickens out as much as possible, and cackle with abandon whenever I see them impale a slug with their ruthless, scaly beaks. Likewise I encourage other predators into the garden (although sadly, I've yet to see a hedgehog). Spotting a blackbird or a thrush gives me a disproportionate amount of pleasure.

I'm aware that I should probably learn to appreciate slugs and snails holistically, as animals playing a vital part in an ecosystem. But I don't. I'm sorry, but I loathe them. Slugs even more than snails, because there's something obscene about a slug. Of course you get big snails too, but at least a snail's got the grace to put itself away once in a while.

It helps if I think of slugs as homeless snails, but only a bit. It seems to me that a slug is a snail with no sense of decency. I swear I saw one on the rain-drenched drive in the autumn that was five inches long and the best part of an inch thick. And a horrible shade of yellow. Slimier than a sideways glance from Piers Morgan, it was.

No, the fact is, we're all living in the wrong county. Or at least, we are if we ever aspire to grow a hosta that doesn't look like Dutch cheese after three minutes of light drizzle. Here in Cornwall, those vile creatures have got us in a horticultural headlock, due to two massive factors in their favour. Firstly, they've got Cornish hedges. I'm surrounded by them, and there's surely no better *des res* for a slug or snail – all shady, dank nooks, crannies and hidey-holes, nestling in between the big, loose stones. A Cornish hedge is a veritable mollusc metropolis. How I dream of owning a plain, well-pointed red brick wall.

Secondly, and most obviously, damp. Cornwall might be paradise, but we all know it can be a drizzly kind of paradise. Slugs and snails love it here as much as we do. Honestly, if I go out in the garden at midnight when it's been raining for a few hours, it's like Piccadilly Circus out there.

Any suggestions for coping with this tsunami of gastropods will be gratefully received. I'm trying not to think of myself as defeated. I will not be broken. I'm training myself to accept them as a necessary evil. Like a gammy leg. Or that little white dog that follows Doc Martin around.

Belonging

2004

P icture the scene. You're Cornish. It's August. You're at a village fete, a couple of miles down the road from where you live. You're with friends, and it's all good fun. You buy some raffle tickets and you have an ice cream. You buy some home-made marmalade from a stall, and after exchanging a bit of small talk with the lady running the stall, you say goodbye. She replies cheerily, "Enjoy the rest of your holiday!"

Right there, in front of everyone, just as you'd been having a perfectly pleasant afternoon, your world collapses around you. Thoughts rush through your head, all at once. Did anybody hear? Did she not notice my accent? How can I put her straight without appearing anally retentive? She may as well have said, "Sorry son, your face just doesn't fit in round here." Who does she think she is anyway? Probably just moved here herself.

So you console yourself with the thought that she's a newcomer to the area, and has no idea that your great, great, great, great grandfather founded the village, (well he could have) and that everyone else within a three-mile radius knows exactly who you are. And yet it knocks you sideways. Truly, there is no more humiliating experience for a Cornishperson than being asked if you're having a nice holiday when you're walking distance from your own front door.

The same thing occurs in other situations. You may be walking along the seafront in a fishing village when some salty old skipper leaning against a railing singles you out and shouts, for all to hear, "Care for a trip round the bay to look for seals?" You look around to check that he was really talking to you. Your mind struggles to compose a withering reply. Something along the lines of: "Actually I was raised by seals, and can still hold my breath underwater for up to twelve minutes". Or perhaps: "Funny you should mention seals my good man – I've just presented my post doctorate treatise on territorial defence mechanisms of male grey seals and related pinnipeds to a convention from the University of Gdansk!" But that would be overreacting. Possibly.

One's thoughts are never quite that composed, alas. Apart from the fact that it might actually be quite nice to have a trip round the bay to see some seals, all you really want to do is shriek "I live here! Can't you tell?"

Many of us are so concerned about this phenomenon that we've developed systems to give out little signs that we live here. On the road the obvious one used to be putting a Kernow sticker on your car, but holidaymakers have caught on to that one. We've also been known to artificially emphasise our accent and vocabulary. For example we might complain loudly in public about the summer crowds, and how it will all be back to normal when the season's over. "Int no room fer parkin' downalong cuz've all they bleddy vizters – 'ave to come back dreckly!" That type of thing. Pity the poor middle class Cornishperson, struggling to assert their validity with no accent to speak of. They're happy to roll the odd 'r' once in a while, and even to chuck in a 'dreckly', or even a 'right on boy'. But they're still living in constant fear of the person they're talking to slowly raising a suspicious eyebrow and saying, knowingly, "That accent. Are you putting that on?"

But when you take a step back, you realise there's really no need to get all hot under the collar about this most peculiar of social conundrums. You just need to take a calm approach. The Cornishperson, confronted by any implication of non-belonging, should simply let out a bellowing guffaw, as loud as possible, immediately followed by a simple, straightforward "Geddon!!" Having practised for several weeks in front of a mirror of course. If executed correctly, the recipient will then spontaneously fall to their knees and exclaim, "My goodness, I'm so sorry, I had no idea you were local. Please accept this pint of ale with my compliments".

I tried it last week. Worked a treat. That woman behind the marmalade stall won't be messing with me again for a while.

Vote

2015

In case you hadn't heard, a vital opportunity presents itself this month. May 7th will hopefully be marking the end of an era – the nation finally has the chance to reject an increasingly untenable state of affairs. It's time to make a difference. Embrace change. This has gone on too long.

I refer, of course, to the mass public vote to choose a National Bird for Britain, which will be culminating on the very same day as the General Election. The robin has been king for almost fifty years, we're told, and it's time to knock our little red-breasted chum off his perch for getting so complacent. The whole thing's being led by naturalist and broadcaster David Lindo. From an original list of sixty, we bird loving Brits have now been given ten to choose from by midnight on May 7th: barn owl, blackbird, blue tit, hen harrier(!), kingfisher, mute swan, puffin, red kite, robin and wren.

Now, if it were a 'Cornwall only' vote, it would be a no brainer (a no *bird* brainer, if you will). Chough. Hands down. Any Cornishperson who thinks otherwise should be forcibly rehomed elsewhere. None of your *'But the chiffchaff is such a delightful little character despite its disappointingly murky plumage'* or *'You simply can't beat a large autumn flock of purple-breasted merganser!'* No, it's got to be the chough – the most beautiful

181

member of the most intelligent family of birds in existence (the corvids), and a supremely aerobatic entertainer. Best of all, it's the sacred bird of Cornwall. For me, only the herring gull comes close. Many of us remember when choughs left us in 1974. Now we've got them back, and we want the world to witness our unerring gratitude. Well, mine anyway.

But I digress, as usual. This isn't about Cornwall, or choughs. It's about the whole of Britain, and our individual reasons for judging one species to be more deserving than another. Presumably the majestic hen harrier is included in the list because it's gorgeous, and very endangered. Quite how it can be compared to the extremely shy and tiny wren, our commonest bird, is anyone's guess. A bit like comparing a lovely bit of stilton with some scrumptious Belgian chocolate.

Anyway, it's all academic. No, not because it's trivial and daft to conduct such a vote on the same day as a General Election (although there is something deliciously, subversively *British* about the timing). But because it's a foregone conclusion. Nothing's ever going to beat a robin in a 'nation's favourite bird' competition. They've got it sewn up.

It's not just the cutesie Christmas card thing, nor the fact that it's so perky, and characterful, and plump, and red-breasted, and tuneful. Sure, these are all points in its favour, but more significantly, robins are Man's Best Friend. Not in a needy way, like a dog, demanding relentless amounts of exercise, and feeding, and paraphernalia, rewarding you only by covering you in saliva, trashing your house and clogging your hoover.

Robins, on the other hand, don't ask for much in return. Most of us garden in some capacity. Even in small urban flats, people find ingenious ways of scratching about on their tiny piece of earth. Bit of weeding, plant a few seeds, you know the kind of thing. And more often than not, what happens? Within minutes, there's a robin, daring to come much closer than is wise, hopping about and chirping, and being generally endearing.

And so brave! A barn owl might be capable of violently ending the lives of several dozen small rodents per night, but it's a right chicken if you go within two hundred yards of it. You'd have your work cut out training a wild barn owl to eat out of your hand, but it's a relatively straightforward exercise with a robin. They're plucky, and they're lovable. Well no, they're hard as nails actually, and well known for fighting to the death over territory. But anthropomorphising them in our usual hubristic way, we find their boldness sweet, because we think it's all about *us*.

Anyway, to vote robin, which you will, simply go to: http://www.votenationalbird.com

It could be the most important thing you do all, well, morning, possibly.

---

* *Guess which bird won. Yep, robin. For the first time in my life I was right about something.*

Authenticity

2014

I t's no good. I've been putting it off for years, but the fact is, my house needs new windows. The existing ones are in a right old state. Almost all of the supposedly 'sealed' window units have sprung a leak, causing condensation within, and giving the steamy impression, from inside the house, of being permanently stuck inside the tropical biome at Eden. It's getting desperate.

I've never liked the cursed things anyway. It's not that I have anything against plastic windows *per se*. Not in a relatively new house, anyway. But mine's not new – it's a really old, cob-and-stone miner's cottage, and no matter how much you squint, plastic windows somehow just look plain wrong.

Whoever it was who saw fit to install them was at least vaguely aware of the history. They nodded in its direction by having white beading put between each double glazed unit, to give the fleeting effect of six little panes of glass. It works, sort of, from a distance. But as the visitor draws closer to the house, the full horror of plastic windows in an otherwise pretty, 250 year old, whitewashed cottage reveals itself. It's like, oh I don't know, putting alloy wheels on your Triumph Vitesse. Or Ikea doorknobs on your regency *armoire*.

But wait a minute. Isn't this quest to preserve the integrity of an old thing all a bit flawed? I mean, just how original do we *really* want things? I'm certain that I don't want to reinstate many things from the mid-eighteenth century into my life. I'm grateful to live in a world with penicillin and the internal combustion engine. Not to mention the bagless vacuum cleaner and the self-erecting, mini beach tent. I'm also grateful to have slates on the roof instead of a thick wodge of straw. And carpet under my feet, instead of bare earth. That's what it would have been like, 250 years ago. Decidedly unpleasant.

I'm quite sure the windows would have been just dreadful back then: rattling, leaking and with a single thin pane of easily broken glass. I'm all for authenticity, but I know my limits. I've got friends renovating a similar house and they've spent years losing sleep, agonizing over how to synchronise 18th century authenticity with 21st century practicality. What style would the radiators have been, for example? Simple answer: "What radiators?"

We unfortunates who choose to dwell in such houses only have ourselves to blame – our angst is entirely self-induced. Old houses can radiate charm, and atmosphere, but it's hard work. Their walls may ooze history, but they ooze quite a few other things too. You're essentially living your life inside the biggest, most expensive antique you'll ever own. And antiques take some looking after. You have to treat them right.

Some people don't even get it anyway. My cousin came over from Canada last year and I could see in his eyes that he was baffled as to why anyone would *opt* to live this way. In fact

I think he went away thinking that the only possible reason for such a choice was that we were poor, and that was the only rational explanation for choosing to live in a house which was, to him, only two steps removed from a cow shed. I think he's got a perfectly valid point.

Anyway, back to the windows. Turns out that all this agonizing is academic anyway. I've started getting quotes for bespoke, small-paned replacement windows that look authentic, original and old, yet at the same time are discreetly double-glazed and efficient. They're coming in at a grand a pop. Talk about ironic – you have to be a millionaire to live like a peasant.

So that's that then. Next time a door-to-door salesman rings the doorbell trying to flog uPVC windows, instead of looking down my nose at him, I'm going to put the kettle on. When I say 'kettle', I'm obviously referring to the old copper one that goes on the top of the woodburner, and not an ugly, inappropriate, new-fangled electric one.

Taxidermy

2017

I used to visit Truro museum at least once a week as a boy. It was only three doors along from my dad's shop, so while I waited for a lift home, I'd often pop in and spend a blissful half hour in the most fantastical world. But please don't think I was cataloguing the admittedly impressive mineralogical specimens. Oh no, I was there for the birds. The stuffed ones.

In through the front door and straight up the grand marble staircase I'd go, taking care not to be spotted glancing at the statue of the naked lady (still there – I checked), and I'd emerge onto the expansive mezzanine level. To a ten year-old boy in 1972 it was a sort of wonderland – case upon case of mounted birds. In my memory there seemed like thousands, but I don't suppose there were actually more than a few dozen.

It's hard to explain the appeal of such a place now, but bear in mind that back then you couldn't go and see a barn owl at Paradise Park, because there was no Paradise Park. Here at the museum I could actually see such a creature, looking *real*. OK, real-*ish*. Quite a few of them were a bit moth-eaten, if I'm honest. The choughs were decidedly skinny, and some of the warblers' plumage had faded to the point where you couldn't really tell the difference. Which, to be honest, rather defeated the object. But in a world where most of the photos in my 1970

Observers Book of Birds were black and white, and tiny, at least these stuffed birds were three-dimensional, life-sized, and, to a degree, coloured.

Taxidermy though – it provokes mixed feelings. There is no doubt that persecution by Man has led to the demise of countless species, and historically our obsession with the stuffing of these species must have contributed significantly. The Cornish chough is a great example. A hundred years ago there weren't many stately homes in Cornwall without a stuffed chough in a glass case proudly displayed on a sideboard somewhere. Only the other day I was at Penlee House in Penzance, and among the olde Cornish displays upstairs, sure enough, there it was: 'Juvenile male chough, shot in Mounts Bay in 1919'. Poor little guy.

But wait a minute. To this day I'm grateful that those stuffed birds were in my local museum. I probably wouldn't love birds now if my interest hadn't been been ignited by that mesmerising collection of specimens. And I'm sure I'm not the only one. Times change. I recently read Chris Packham's inspirational autobiography. It turns out that as a boy, he had a spectacular collection of birds' eggs, some of them very rare. He knows now that it was wrong, and yet sourcing, researching, obtaining and curating those eggs played an integral part in him becoming the brilliant TV presenter, photographer and naturalist he is today.

These days, we live in comparatively enlightened times. Truro museum is very 21st century now, and while there's arguably little place for a parade of dusty old stuffed birds, some of the better specimens have been cleverly recycled and incorporated into rather nice 'Cornish habitat' displays: coastal, heathland, that kind of thing. I'm happy to say that even the three (yes, *three*) stuffed choughs have a display all of their own, celebrating their triumphant return to Cornwall and current glorious resurgence. Deeply ironic, yes, but at least they've been put to good use.

And now, perhaps surprisingly, I'm told that taxidermy's having a revival, in the form of something called '*rogue taxidermy*'. This apparently involves the 21st century taxidermist adopting a Dali-esque approach to his/her craft, actually amalgamating elements of different animals. It's a lot more politically correct now, of course – animals are more sustainably sourced, ideally dying from natural causes (or road traffic accidents probably). Apparently in 2017 no hipster worth his organic, hand-harvested sea salt would be seen dead without a responsibly sourced fox's head, sporting a pair of muntjac deer antlers, adorning the exposed brick walls of his loft apartment.

Funny how things move on.

Annuals

2003

This time of year, with spring upon us, we British gardeners start to get carried away with new ideas. It's not our fault – it's the feel of a bit of warm sun on our skin, the clocks changing, and all those inspiring articles they start putting in the Sunday supplements. We cut the lawn for the first time, the Chelsea Flower Show looms and our seed trays are bursting with little bundles of joy just itching to be planted out so they can show us what they've got. But be warned, I have a cautionary tale to tell.

At the beginning of last year there was a large, sunny, sheltered, herbaceous border at the front of my house. Years of neglect and my horticultural incompetence had turned the border into a huge clump, turgid with anonymous perennials, all in drastic need of dividing, or better still, killing. In amongst all this were deep-rooted thickets of couch grass and dock. It was a vile mess. I deliberated for a good long time, then finally summoned up the courage to do something about it.

So I yanked the whole lot out. I took care to remove any bits of root remaining in the soil. I waited for the second flush of weeds, and weeded again. Then I dug in lots of compost, and raked it to a fine tilth. Just like you're supposed to. Looking at my now clean, virgin plot I stood, Monet-like, and painted in my mind swathes of technicolour floribundance. Toying with the idea of an actual colour scheme, I read somewhere that muted, subtle colours were no longer in fashion, and that it was now quite acceptable to bung in whatever colours you wanted, in a more *naturalistic* approach to planting. That's handy, I thought. I had visions of friends dropping by and standing, slack-jawed, in awe. Photographers would arrive, begging me to allow them to try to capture this sublime example of the art, and by May people would be walking around Chelsea exclaiming: "Well this is all very nice, but I haven't seen anything here that can hold a candle to that stunning border we saw in Cornwall!"

But first I had to plant something. I'd experimented with different kinds of plants in other parts of the garden – a group of succulents here, an attempt at a shrubbery there. I'd actually become clinically addicted to attending plant auctions, where amazing bargains were to be had (as long as you weren't too concerned what type of plant you were actually buying). My wife's wise words, "It's only a bargain if you need it," had fallen on deaf ears time and time again, as I'd arrive home with a car packed full of seventy-five bare root escallonias of dubious heritage. "I got them for four quid. I'm going to plant a hedge," I'd say, unconvincingly, desperately racking my brains for somewhere needing a hundred yard windbreak. But in the case of this particular border, I rather fancied trying something new.

As usual there were endless articles appearing in the Sunday supplements about what can be achieved with annuals, these plants that gave it their all, growing from seed to flower in one season, and going out in a blaze of glory. Cheap and easy, drifts of cottage-style colour throughout the season, the magazines said. Pictures of stunning cottagey borders all grown from less than a fiver's worth of seeds. I'd always wanted to try an annual border, so resolved to give it a go. Carefully I started sowing drifts of hardy annuals in late March, and cleverly raised more tender ones indoors, ready to be planted out when it got a bit warmer. I couldn't have been more prepared.

What I hadn't counted on was that spring didn't arrive til August. For four months it all looked terrible. Still more weeds came – a third flush. My tiny, carefully thinned seedlings fought for dominance over far tougher native weeds. But weeds weren't the real problem. The real problem was the weather. As 'spring' turned into 'summer' my pathetic crop fought for its very life in what was rapidly becoming a muddy quagmire of Tolkeinesque proportions. With virtually no sunshine and clobbered by rain, incessant wind and well below average temperatures, nothing had even got close to forming a flower by the beginning of July. We were well into barbecue season, the evenings were starting to get shorter and my dream border remained more aspirational than inspirational. It was embarrassing. Just how long was I supposed to wait?

Then, during July, a little hoped bloomed. A few brave plants made a mad, desperate lunge at showing us what they could do. I made a point of thanking every one personally. An isolated little group of love-in-a-mist looked nice, at least the ones that were still vertical. So too did the gypsophyla, though they only lasted a week. Some slightly alarming thirty-inch high cornflowers made an appearance, and immediately got clobbered by a gale. Tall, majestic spikes of larkspur finally bloomed and looked lovely. But there were only the three of them. More a modest grouping than what Gertrude Jekyll might have called a *swathe*.

So by the end of the 'growing season' last year, the most impressive elements in my annual border were some pretty red poppies (no idea where they came from as I certainly hadn't planted them), and a rather arresting display of scarlet pimpernel. Recalling that a weed is any plant growing in the wrong place, and this scarlet pimpernel looked about as good as anything I'd grown intentionally, I left it. It looked quite spectacular for a while. Thank goodness for weeds. The photographers didn't come, and visitors didn't comment. Well not in a positive way anyway. Quite a few people said something like, "Oh dear, what's happened here?"

By October, as I stood there and gazed upon what might have been, and reflected on the shame it had brought upon me, I thought about what I'd learned from it all. Like Lear emerging from the storm, I saw things in a whole new light. The thing about gardening is you've got to put the hours in. No matter how easy and straightforward that nice Titchmarsh chap makes it sound, at the end of the day there's an awful lot of fiddly attention to detail involved in growing things.

Choosing a slightly more sheltered site might not have been such a bad idea. "And you could have used canes for support,"

I hear you cry. Yet I just didn't want to get into that, because although it's OK for the odd sunflower, tying up every individual plant over eighteen inches just seemed to defeat the whole object of a natural-looking border.

I should have admitted to myself that few things in life these days are as natural as they seem. A faded pair of jeans didn't get like that in the wash! They've been bought like that, faded to just the right level for this year's fashion. If only I'd taken my cue from that teenager I observed at the mirror in my local pub Gents the other night. He didn't get that completely natural, just-got-out-of-bed-and-don't-give-a-damn look just by getting out of bed and not giving a damn. No, he had to stand there like a fool carefully teasing bits of meticulously-gelled hair into just the right position. You can learn from the oddest teachers.

The fact is that none of this tweaking and preening is for me. I've had it with annuals. This year I'm re-embracing the world of proper plants. Decent plants. Herbaceous perennials. Plants which live for more than a year, don't lie down and die at the first sign of a light breeze and can be propagated with the aid of a hefty whack with a dirty spade. That's my kind of plant. An annual is a fickle friend. A perennial is a gift that keeps on giving. Forget gypsophyla, I'm growing geraniums.

Besides, I just bought a job lot of twenty miscellaneous perennials without labels in an auction. Only a tenner. Bargain.

Kylie Poldark

2016

S o, another year over, and the world seems to be changing faster than ever. But although it often feels as if we're on another planet compared with forty years ago, there's one small respect in which 2016 is feeling an awful lot like 1976. *Poldark* fever is back. In a big way.

It's every bit as big as it was back when the first version aired in the seventies, and I can't be the only one feeling a comforting sense of déjà vu. Although I still know a handful of people who refuse to watch it for one reason or another, it's affected all of us in some way: the palpable increase in tourist numbers, the constant buzz about filming locations, not to mention the welcome boost in revenue (everything from increased book sales to the tackiest tourist tat). The *Poldark* vibe really is tangible.

I expect the next thing we'll be noticing is little Demelzas popping up all over the place. It happened in the seventies, and these days we seem even more inclined to name our kids after whoever takes our fancy off the telly, from *Game of Thrones* characters to members of *One Direction*. So I'd be amazed if the September 2021 intake of girls at Cornish primary schools doesn't feature a healthy smattering of Demelzas. You mark my words.

Demelza's all very well. It's only existed as a girl's name since the book came out in 1950, and was only significantly adopted by people from the late seventies onwards. But what of the other Poldarky names? For some reason the name Ross never caught on in the same way as Demelza. I certainly don't expect to be meeting a lot of Unwins anytime soon, but that's more to do with the fact that Unwin Trevaunance was a twit.

But I've been thinking about the name *Jeremy*. With series two at an end, Ross and Demelza's new son is well and truly on the scene, and, without wanting to issue any spoiler alerts, I think it's safe to say that he's *significant*. However, the name *Jeremy* sits a little uncomfortably these days – it's not a name you traditionally associate with heroes, is it? These days it seems a curious name for Winston Graham to have chosen for Ross Poldark's progeny.

Or is it? When you stop to think about it, a lot of Jeremies are not very Jeremy-like at all. They're people you wouldn't mess with. Several spring easily to mind. There's Paxman, obviously, and Jeremy Kyle. There's Jeremy Guscott, one of the greatest centres to ever wear an England shirt. Ah, and Jeremy Bowen, the coolest man on the telly, the very essence of articulate calm, standing in front of the camera, day after day, reporting from some ghastly war zone, all open shirted, as relaxed as a *Shearings* coach tour guide. Jeremy Clarkson needs no introduction. And say what you like about Corbyn, he's held onto his position as Labour leader despite what once seemed like overwhelming odds against him. They don't come any more tenacious.

It was sixty-six years ago that Winston Graham decided to name the character *Jeremy*. It was a relatively popular name back then. By 2009 it had plummeted to a lowly 417th position in the UK new babies list. Depending on what becomes of Jeremy Poldark (and I couldn't possibly say), I reckon a resurgence of Jezzers-es could definitely be on the cards.

When, at a book launch in 2002, the great author quietly mentioned to my wife that he was considering her name, Becky, for a character in his next *Poldark* book, it was a spine-tingling moment. To be honest, he was such a twinkly-eyed, charming man that he'd probably have told her the same thing if her name had been Kylie (I'm not going to tell her that, because the thought still thrills her to this day). Anyway we'll never know, because he passed away the following year, and the book never came. But the thought of having a *Poldark* character named after you, rather than the other way round, is quite something.

I reckon that might even beat getting a selfie with Aidan Turner.

Family holiday

2013

Hmm. This parenthood business is all a bit tricky, isn't it? Since the momentous day five years ago when the missus and I turned, overnight, into a family of four, life has become rather more complicated. No, *infinitely* more complicated. Being responsible for two little five-year-old boys makes you reassess every single aspect of your world. Constantly.

Holidays are a good example. I've always had a somewhat relaxed attitude when it comes to going away. In my twenties and thirties, working freelance, my world was so unstructured that I used to find myself going without a holiday for ages, and then setting off backpacking for months at a time. Oh, to live life with such reckless abandon now.

In the five years since I became a family man, we've been too tired to think seriously about a proper, organised, 'family' holiday. Besides, there's never seemed much point, because how much does anyone remember about the first five years of their life? What's the point in taking infants to some exotic destination if they aren't going to remember a thing about it? Mere self-indulgence on the parents' part if you ask me. In fact young children are well known for their endearing habit of recalling the minutiae of an experience and completely missing the supposed point of the thing. Thus when we took the boys to the Natural History Museum, the amazing, robotic, life-sized dinosaurs were spurned in favour of the busker's hat in the subway on the way there. Take them to the zoo and they'll more than likely look past the lions at a particularly squidgy looking slug. Dear of 'em.

Any remote hankering for an ambitious holiday has, until now, conjured up visions of the four of us, tired and teary, in some awful departure lounge, fighting with foreign bureaucracy, elusive toilets and sleep deprivation, arriving home even more exhausted than when we left, thus defeating the whole object. So we've spent the last five years burying our heads in the sand, managing only spontaneous camping trips to some of the more far-flung corners of Cornwall. I've watched, open mouthed in awe, as countless friends gamely cart their under fives off to foreign resorts, theme parks, who knows where else. Sensational news items about high achieving five-year-olds climbing Kilimanjaro don't help.

Until now. For now the boys are five, and the fact is, we do need to get away, go somewhere, do something new. I can't keep using the same old excuse that we live in the UK's premier holiday destination. Tight, lazy Cornishpeople like me have been trotting that one out for too long. We need to go to a well-chosen destination that we'll all appreciate, and, who knows, may even become the boys' first proper, bona-fide memory. But the whole thing's thrown me into very unfamiliar territory. What an ordeal it all is! And how the very concept of a holiday has changed since my carefree backpacking days.

The whole thing is a logistical minefield. And there's the annoying irony that while they are now old enough to enjoy a proper holiday, we are now restricted horribly by school holidays.

And inexplicably, the price of everything doubles in the school holidays. Triples, even. I've never had to factor that in before! A week's modest camping in France requires a budget roughly equivalent to four months' living expenses last time I went backpacking. It's crazy. I used to spend £50 transporting my motorcycle across the channel. Now, for a family or four in a flipping great estate car with bicycles strapped to the back and a huge plastic pod on the roof, it costs ten times that just to get from Plymouth to Roscoff. I tell you, it's all come as a bit of a shock.

If we don't pull our finger out soon, it's looking like another Cornish camping sojourn for us. I'll tell you one thing though – we're not going to Disneyland. I've already been there. I was 28 and single. Brilliant it was.

Space race

2016

W ell, you could have knocked me down with a high-energy particle detector last month when I heard the latest news about Newquay. There can't have been many of us who saw that one coming. If you remember, the government confirmed its support for the development of Britain's first spaceport, and was apparently looking for a site from which paying punters and satellites will be launched into orbit. Along with four contender sites in Scotland and one in Wales, is......wait for it.....little ol' Newquay airport. If you can't quite believe what you just read, here it is again in a nutshell: *Spaceport*. In *Newquay*.

When I heard 'Newquay' and 'space' in the same sentence, all that came to mind was a distant memory of watching live coverage of the 1970 Apollo 13 mission, huddled round Auntie Dolly's black and white telly in her Newquay bungalow. Beyond that, it had never really occurred to me to put the two together. Why would you? I mean, Newquay airport? Humble little St Mawgan? Really?

Well yes, actually. The basic facts of this Newquay space bid, once digested, make perfect sense: it has one of the longest runways in the country, it's right by the Atlantic Ocean, and there's a long established airport there already. And it's only forty minutes from London, and apparently there's lots of available land.

But I need to stop calling it *St Mawgan*. No-one calls it that anymore. Not the civilian bit anyway. Just as we now call Truro City Hall the *Hall for Cornwall*, and Treliske Hospital the *Royal Cornwall Hospital*, St Mawgan is '*Cornwall Airport Newquay*', and has been for some time. Everything rebrands eventually, I suppose. It's part of staying in business. But this goes way beyond a mere new name. *Cornwall Airport Newquay* is part of a whole new business concept called *Aerohub*, which is an '*aerospace enterprise zone*'. To be honest I'm always nervous of anything with 'hub' in its title, but this idea looks like futuristic thinking, offering companies all the advantages of being right next to the county's most significant airport. With zero business rates, apparently. And superfast broadband, obviously. Surely that's good news for one of the poorest counties in the country.

To be honest, I was barely aware that things at Newquay airport had changed this dramatically. It's years since I've even been up there, although last time I visited I do remember everyone getting quite hot under the collar about having to pay a £5 '*airport development fee*'. And I was vaguely aware of building work going on. But observing one's surroundings was always a hard job in the face of disembarking metrosexual Londoners wielding vast surfboard bags and frenziedly jostling for a taxi to rush them to Jamie Oliver's Watergate Bay restaurant for a time slot that their over optimistic secretary had considered perfectly do-able that afternoon. And if you didn't get smacked in the face by an 8ft mini-mal, the hordes of embarking scarlet stag weekend refugees would probably get you instead. I realise now that the building work I glimpsed was part of some serious reconstruction.

Whether Newquay wins the race to become Britain's first spaceport or not, you can't fail to be impressed, and even just bidding for it is a serious headline grabber. There's also a rather delicious paradox here. For as long as any of us can remember, people have flocked down here to Cornwall, Britain's premier holiday destination. With its huge range of gorgeous beaches pointing in all directions, Newquay has arguably been the jewel in that crown. And now there is a real possibility that there will be holidaymakers arriving in Newquay, then paying seriously big bucks for the privilege of being blasted a very long distance away from it.

End of an era

2013

Last year, Cornwall lost two unique personalities. This couple had moved here with a friend in 2001, making their home down on the Lizard. As soon as I met them eleven years ago, I knew they were special. I wasn't the only one – plenty felt the same way. Their very appearance in Cornwall changed everything. They were *that* important. But little did we know what they would go on to achieve.

Overnight, they made the place feel a whole lot more, well, *Cornish*. Although their friend disappeared up the coast to do her own thing, the couple settled on the Lizard, and the following year started raising a family. They were truly two of the most charismatic characters I've ever met.

We became firm friends, and we saw a lot of each other, mostly in the spring and summer, when they didn't travel too far from their cave. My very first article in this magazine was about them. I wrote a children's book, giving them the names Dirak and Bir (Breton names, because at the time we thought that's where they were from). And now they're gone. Dirak died violently in a terrible fight. Bir stayed around for a week or two after that, and then disappeared. No-one's seen her since. Choughs pair for life you see. It's quite possible that she just pined away.

Ah, but what a legacy those two birds left us. Unbelievably, they raised a family every year for twelve consecutive years – an incredible feat. They successfully fledged 44 chicks, single-handedly reinstating Cornwall's most culturally significant bird. Thanks to those two birds, there are choughs dotted all along the west Cornwall coastline. And now Dirak and Bir's offspring are continuing to recolonise Cornwall with a healthy chough population. 101 chough chicks are known to have fledged here since 2001. But it was that pioneering pair who worked the hardest.

I remember the stunning summer's day in 2002 when I was determined to get some decent photos of them, lugging all my camera equipment for miles with Stuart Croft, the original RSPB chough protection officer. They eluded us for hours, then out of the blue just swooped in and landed right next to us on the coast path, too close for my big camera lens to focus. By the time I'd clumsily got a new lens set up, they'd gone, and I didn't know whether to curse them or admit that it had been a wonderful, spontaneously intimate experience.

There was the Sunday afternoon in February 2008 when I took my month-old twin boys down to Southerly Point to show them choughs for the first time, and the wind and rain were so vicious you could barely open the car door. Nothing was flying in that, or so I thought. I managed to get out of the car, and stood alone in the car park clutching the railing for dear life, when I heard a big flock of jackdaws. They flew low, right through me, and in among the jackdaws I counted twelve choughs – the most I've ever seen at the same time in

205

Cornwall. Oh, and the afternoon in 2003 when we held a first birthday party for the previous year's fledglings on the terrace at the Southerly Point Café and the new family flew past us so low we swore they were after a piece of their own birthday cake. And there have been all the nest watch shifts for the RSPB, day and night. Special times.

Dirak and Bir perished in June last year. We've known for years that it was going to happen, and now it has, and I still can't quite believe it. But this is nature. Life goes on. A new breeding season is looming, and the sacred cave where they raised all those youngsters, year after year, may be used by new choughs (in fact the chough that finished off Dirak is showing promising signs of moving into the old nest). That would be great. We all know that the important thing is to keep increasing the population.

But it will never quite be the same.

Queue

2015

W hat do you reckon is the single most significant characteristic that makes us all *British*?

Our outdated notion of *Empire* perhaps? Or our unique sense of humour, as demonstrated in such iconic TV comedy classics as *Fawlty Towers*, or these days the loveable and self-deprecating *Miranda*? Or could it be our endearing ability to celebrate failure? We do, after all, recall the name of hopeless but loveable wannabe sportsman Eddie the Eagle long before those of actual successful athletes from the 1988 Winter Olympics (go on – just try). Victors are great, but winning is all a bit, well, *obvious*, really, isn't it? A bit showy-offy. We Brits much prefer a plucky *also ran*.

All worthy contenders, but no, it is none of these. The single most significant thing that makes us uniquely British is our innate and obsessive love of *queuing*. Wherever you see two British strangers standing, simply add a third and they will, by definition, re-assemble themselves in the order in which they arrived at the scene. It's only right. It creates order from chaos. How we Brits do love to queue. It shows us, quite literally, where we all stand.

There are exceptions though. I can think of three social situations where, for no obvious reason, we do not queue, but probably should, because not doing so makes us very uncomfortable. First, there's the confusing world that is the chip shop. On arrival, you have the daunting job of finding your place among customers who've already ordered, and those waiting to order, all of whom are standing apparently randomly about the place. You can only bide your time, and hope that by quietly monitoring the situation, some sort of system might reveal itself.

Then there's the barber's shop. These would be infinitely less stressful places if all the chaps just sat down in order and moved along one when a customer stood up to sit in the barber's chair. But no. When you walk in, you have to sit on any available chair, then set about memorizing all the other faces in the room, as well as keeping tabs on who arrives after you. And you have to do all this while looking like you couldn't care less, or it wouldn't be British. It ain't easy.

But most significant of all is the pub. Here we observe the most challenging of social structures. On arrival at the bar, we take a cursory glance at who's already waiting, then assume the position, and set about catching the barperson's eye.

If you are knowingly served before someone who got there first, you have the opportunity to gallantly say to your rival: "I think you were before me?" thus garnering the respect of all onlookers (but risking remaining thirsty for another ten minutes, having missed your chance). This grand gesture is usually only witnessed if *a)* the other waiting person looks like they might punch your lights out, *b)* you know the person, or *c)* you fancy the person. Otherwise, I'd say this is arguably the one social situation in Britain where it is perfectly permissible to push in.

Ah, but here's the thing. Last summer I witnessed something incredible. It happened before my very eyes in my local pub, on several occasions, and I've never seen the like before in this country. I'm baffled. There, at the crowded bar, among the customers waiting to be served, *a queue formed*. One person decided, quite spontaneously, that rather than jostle for position at the bar, they'd prefer to wait politely behind the person being served. And then more joined. Imagine! Who would do this? Someone so overwhelmed by their very *Britishness* that they simply couldn't help themselves? Queuing is, after all, in our DNA. Or was it being instigated by a confused holidaymaker? Possibly an American tourist, trying to join in with one of our national obsessions, but tragically choosing to queue (or 'line up' as he'd probably say) in one of the only situations when we don't.

Whatever the reason, I'm wondering if it's going to happen again once the holiday season kicks in and things get a bit busy. Please keep an eye out, and feel free to report back.

The smallest coin

2007

There's a great Charles Causley poem called *'A Visit to Stratford'*, in which Causley describes travelling up to Shakespeare's birthplace. The poet is seeking inspiration, hoping that soaking up some bardy vibes might somehow act as a set of existential jumpleads. He finds no such inspiration, and returns, dejected, back home to Cornwall. Only then, at the end of the poem, as Causley slumps in front of the fire in his own sitting room, does he see the light, in the form of Shakespeare's own words, staring him in the face the whole time:

> *'Why do you travel so far for what is most near?*
> *The smallest coin in your purse buys what is most dear.'*

A useful lesson. But don't get me wrong – I'm all for exotic travel. I wouldn't have missed seeing the mountain gorillas in Uganda's Bwindi Impenetrable Forest, nor the midnight sun in the Alaskan Arctic. But just as Shakespeare tells us, the real life-affirming experiences often come much closer to home. Especially if home's Cornwall.

My most recent coast path walk is a fine example. The missus and I have been methodically trudging the whole Cornish section of this national treasure, bit by bit. We'd been needing to complete the top section, right on the Devon border, so we put aside four days, and aimed to get the Hartland Quay to Tintagel leg done in one go.

On the first day, just over the Devon border, we saw a hare. OK, it might not have the kudos of a humpback whale, but it's the first time this Cornish boy had ever seen one, and that means it's the first new indigenous British mammal I've seen for, well, decades! Plainly bigger than your average rabbit, it looked right at us, then eventually lurched off on its lanky legs. The trip was worth it just for that. And it was only the first morning!

I'd assumed that this 'upcountry' section would be rather more built up than the parts I'm more familiar with down west. After all, we're talking about the border of Devon, that scary county that has proper cities, and a motorway an' all. But we were amazed to find that it felt more remote than any equivalent section of the coast path so far. And the topography was a surprise too. Sheer, sharp cliffs of dead straight black slate at amazing angles, and beaches with endless striations of the same stuff, stretching out to sea. So different to the landscape we're used to further west.

After three hours we entered our fine and noble Duchy, the event marked by the smallest wooden bridge placed over a trickling stream, and a discreet sign saying, simply, 'Cornwall'. At Morwenstow we entered the world of the eccentric 19th century Parson Hawker. We sat in the little lookout hut he'd built from driftwood, from where the charismatic parson would sit in his cassock and woolly jumper, scanning the landscape for shipwrecks so that he could honour those poor lost souls with a decent burial. It wasn't hard to imagine him perched there scribbling verse and taking the occasional draw on his opium pipe (or completely off his face, depending on which literature you choose to take seriously).

After that it was more world-class scenery, including a view of the Coombe valley with Kilkhampton Church in the distance which I reckon rivalled anything in the *Lord of the Rings* films. Then on to Bude, where we stocked up on second-hand books and enjoyed the best curry we've had since we lived in curry-laden south London. Next day it was a killer seventeen-miler involving scenery so diverse that it ranged from the heathland of Dartmoor to the turquoise waters of Zanzibar to the dramatic river valleys of New Zealand's south island. Eventually it brought us, dead on our feet, into the gorgeous and unique Boscastle, mid-evening. We found a B&B run by the loveliest couple who'd just celebrated their diamond wedding anniversary, then staggered to the nearest pub, where the fish supper was as you would always like it to be, but seldom is: genuinely fresh, big, and thankfully devoid of a silly, freezing-cold 'salad garnish'.

Next day the short hop to the Tintagel finish, and another wildlife highlight – pausing not far out of Boscastle to enjoy the seabird havens of Long and Short Rock, and watching the auks doing their thing. And then, out flying low amongst the guillemots and the razorbills, there it was. So far out that to have lowered our binoculars we'd have lost it forever, but unmistakable with its spectacular parrot bill: a puffin. The first I've ever seen in the south west outside of Scilly.

And we were there. A thousand landscapes absorbed, another 36 miles ticked off, countless lessons learned. At one point I did question the validity of Shakespeare's *"Smallest coin in your purse buys what is most dear"*, as four nights in a B&B for two actually required a purse full of rather large coins. But who cares – that's not the point. I can't remember ever spending a more worthwhile four days anywhere in the world. How I love Cornwall. Devon's not so bad either, come to that.

Bah! Humbuggery

2014

As always, I'm looking forward to Christmas. The thought of all the usual lovely traditions are already filling me with a familiar sense of anticipation. There'll be our annual visit to the lights at Angarrack, that modest yet always impressive alternative to the bun fight at Mousehole. There'll be the look on the children's faces, the relaxing down-time, the excuse to indulge in things that for the rest of the year would be considered self-indulgent: presents, overeating, alcohol abuse, watching telly.

Cue that sound effect with the gramophone needle scratching across a record. The thing is, it's never really like that is it? For me at least, the anticipation of Christmas always seems to exceed the actual event, because it is always so relentlessly, mind numbingly, *frantic*. It doesn't help that my twin boys' birthday comes three days after Christmas Day. This transforms what could otherwise be a joyful, relaxed, family celebration into four days of sustained mania. Four days of piling up bin bags stuffed with discarded wrapping paper, and making endless lists of who-gave-what-to-whom so that we can have a vague stab at some thank-you letters at some point, and general mayhem. And in amongst all this, one is expected to cook the most impressive meal of the year, and arrange a large party for a couple of dozen hyped-up children. The two most significant days of my children's year, falling within three days of each other. Multiplied by two. Honestly, I'm shaking already.

But please don't think I'm just blaming my innocent infants for my miserable *humbuggery*. It is, after all, absolutely not their fault. And anyway, Christmas has always been like this for me. Ever since I can remember, there's never been any time to relax. My parents (and my grandfather before that) owned a toyshop. A big one, right in the middle of Truro, called *Rickards* (oh and in case you're thinking that I must have had my pick of fabulous presents from the toyshop, I didn't. But I'll save that particular hangup for another time). It was before the big chain stores started putting all the little guys out of business with their 'Pile 'em high, sell 'em cheap' ethos, and throughout most of the twentieth century, people came from all over the place to my folks' shop for their toys. We sold a big range of prams and pushchairs too. Christmas, inevitably, was a crazy time. It was all hands on deck, and the whole family was roped in to work.

The only plus side was that in the buildup to Christmas we'd sometimes get to eat out in a Chinese restaurant as Mother was too busy to cook tea, and the taste of sweet and sour pork, to this eight year-old Cornish boy in 1970, was exotic and sublime. Right through December, the shop got busier as people flocked to buy Dinky toys and Pelham puppets and Sindy dolls and Hornby trainsets, until Christmas Day finally arrived. My dad was broken, and how my mother summoned up any inclination to cook a huge, extravagant

215

lunch, I've no idea. The Christmas break wasn't so much a period of celebration, as one of recuperation.

The shop's long gone now, but all these years later, things aren't that much different, and my feelings towards the impending festive season are, let's just say, *ambivalent*. I'm sure I'm not the only one. And it goes on so long! We were still in shorts when we noticed the frenzied Christmas shelf stacking in supermarkets and garden centres, so by the beginning of December we're already at fever pitch, and by Christmas Day we've lost the will to live.

And yet when we look back at Christmases past, it is with affection. Our happy memories always seem to cancel out the exhaustion, the family tensions, and, hopefully, the debt, and we only recall the good stuff. Christmas really is the triumph of hope over experience, and I'm glad for it. Bring it on.

So I'll end by saying, and I mean this fairly sincerely, HAPPY CHRISTMAS.

Pipe

2004

I turned forty a couple of years ago.

It wasn't too bad, all things considered. I've always looked fairly young for my age, and had spent the first thirty years wishing I looked older, then went through this sort of transitional period when I realised that gravity and three curries a week had begun to take a cruel toll. I then settled into the more traditional middle-aged man's pangs of regret that I hadn't taken better care of myself. All fairly textbook stuff. I was OK with it. But something happened last week that terrified me. No, not my first heart murmur. And it wasn't the discovery that I could no longer see my feet. It was more tragic and shocking than either of those. I saw someone I went to school with, *smoking a pipe*.

He wasn't messing around either. This was real thing: a proper, big, bona-fide, briar pipe. You know, the sort your grandad used to smoke. And you know what? He looked good. It suited him. People weren't giggling and whispering "Look at that silly young man. Doesn't he realise pipes are for grown ups?" People weren't looking at him at all. He just looked like a middle-aged bloke with a pipe. He looked very comfortable with it, like he'd been doing it for some time. Maybe he'd been smoking it for years!

I tried to convince myself it was simply a case of mistaken identity. Maybe it wasn't him at all, but his much older brother, in his late fifties, or some haggard doppelganger – I did read somewhere that we all have one somewhere, in some parallel universe. But it was unlikely that said doppelganger would show up within ten miles of where you'd both gone to school. I certainly wasn't going to go and confront him to confirm his identity. Not after he'd humiliated me like this.

So I admitted to myself that it was definitely him. And the reality was unnerving. At eighteen, I'd worried about being asked my age in a pub. At thirty I was worried that my career was going to tie me to London and prevent me from getting back to Cornwall for the rest of my life. At forty I'd learned that someone from school had become a grandparent. Oh yes, I'd experienced my fair share of ageing anxiety. But this was so much worse. This was personal.

Yet as I sat there, at a comfortable distance so as not to be spotted, but close enough to observe him, I got to thinking, perhaps it's not such a problem after all. Perhaps I simply associate pipe smoking with old people because my main frame of reference is my dad, who I always remember with a pipe sticking out of his mouth, and who I always remember as, well, *old*. You don't really see a lot of chaps smoking a pipe nowadays – they seem to exist in some lost PG Wodehouse world where men wore plus fours, and drove one of those Inspector Morse Jags with a golden retriever lying in the back on a red tartan blanket. A world with train compartments full of thick, carcinogenic fug, and childhood memories of Sunday afternoon drives to Perranporth sitting in the back seat, passively inhaling great lungfuls of your dad's pipe smoke. You saw a lot of pipes back then.

I decided to talk to Mother about it (I couldn't discuss it with my dad, because he died years ago (at 59, from lung cancer, funnily enough). We worked out that he'd been somewhere in the vicinity of thirty-three when he made the switch from fags to pipe, and became a real man. This revelation came as some considerable relief to me. All was well! Pipe smoking was a young man's game after all. I'd been remembering all pipe smokers as old, purely because I'd been *young*. A pipe wasn't the grim harbinger of impending dotage at all. It was just another phase that one went through as one approached middle age. And so I concluded that the 'Pipe Age' was no big deal. I've even considered getting one myself. But I reckon I'm a bit old for it now.

Battery hens

2014

T he last of our chickens died a few months back, which led myself and the missus to do some thinking. We wanted to get some more, but we fancied a change – our last lot of hens had been proper posh, from a specialist breeder, with a price tag to match. This time, we were going to do something a little more noble.

We'd often heard people waxing lyrical about the joys of acquiring ex-battery hens (actually I believe ex-'caged' hens is the correct term these days). So we got in touch with the *British Hen Welfare Trust*, went on their list, and waited to be contacted next time they rescued a batch. After a few weeks we received an email, telling us where to be on a certain date.

Heading for the designated address to pick up our consignment of abused chickens one sunny Sunday, I had no idea who else might be there – middle class *Guardian* readers in German estate cars, all self-righteously 'doing their bit'? Old vans full of well-meaning hippy vegetarians? I mean, who does this sort of thing? As it turned out, we were the only ones there, so I'll never know. There, in a big shed, was the reason we'd come: 150 bewildered 'ex-batts'. What a sad sight these little creatures were. Half bald, they'd never set one foot in front of the other, and to be honest, didn't look like they ever would. Skin and bone, with occasional tufts of manky ginger feathers, they'd never seen the sky, or rain, or grass, or any other type of animal. We were swiftly given our six hens, and bundled them into boxes.

Arriving home, we carefully removed the lids and discovered that two of them had laid us an egg already, dear of them. We couldn't help letting hubris get the better of us, imagining that they'd started laying eggs as soon as possible to say 'thank you'. In reality of course they didn't have a clue what was going on, let alone how lucky they were. Next day when we lifted them out of the hen house for the first time, they just stood there. They had no idea what to do.

But they soon learned, and within a day or two were behaving like normal chickens – scratching around, making contented clucking sounds, and establishing a pecking order. As the weeks went by, they became increasingly endearing. I'll never forget watching them cocking their heads to watch a flock of rooks flying overhead for the first time. Or when they first experienced rain, and just stood there staring. They're easy to catch and pick up (a big advantage when you're trying to convince a six-year-old to think of them as a pet). Truly, these hens are a gift that keeps on giving. I really can't recommend ex-batt hens highly enough.

If we hadn't rescued them, these animals would no doubt have been ground up in some ghastly product, bringing to an end a sad and worthless life. These sweet little creatures would have spent 18 months as practically motionless egg-laying machines, then destroyed. We all know it, yet we're complicit.

We humans consider the poor, degraded chicken as a barely sentient thing. I always try to buy good meat, but I'm not going to make a nuisance of myself demanding to know its provenance every time I order a chicken jalfrezi. So I'm as guilty as anyone.

I'll be the first to admit that 'rescuing' six chickens hasn't changed anything. It hasn't made the slightest dent in humans' merciless exploitation of, well, everything worth exploiting. But it genuinely has, in a small way, changed my family for the better. My boys have learned a bit about responsibility – collecting eggs every day, checking the hens for mites, and mucking out twice a week. Who cares if what we've done has made absolutely no difference in the general scheme of things? Six servile creatures have in some tiny way benefitted from the fact that the human race is capable of kindness as well as relentless abuse. Although I'm still no vegetarian, I honestly do feel like a fractionally better person. That's got to be worth something, surely.

There's one problem though. Consuming and distributing three dozen eggs a week is no joke.

Fitting in 4: Bare feet

2013

I've received quite a bit of correspondence over the years regarding my occasional efforts to help the incomer to Cornwall fit in. So here's a bit more useful advice. This short course of self-help classes will thus be at an end, and I expect to be noticing a significant improvement around Cornwall in the coming months. That means no-one trying to look the part by wearing shorts in winter, sunglasses at night, or those pastel coloured rugby-style shirts with the collar turned up.

Right. There's one more thing that instantly marks people out as an incomer/holidaymaker trying a bit too hard. It is *the inappropriate display of bare feet.*

Now, I'd be the first to admit that when the weather's hot, there's nothing nicer than letting the air circulate around those pinkies. After all, the poor things spend practically their whole life containerised in a world of fetid airlessness. Little wonder in those stinking petri dishes we call shoes they fall prey to so many disgusting disorders. So like most other parts of the body, as long as the weather's playing along, I'm all for giving them a good airing.

However, it's amazing how many people you see taking this to a ridiculous extreme. All I'm saying is, please, *a)* not outdoors in January, *b)* not in Tescos, and *c)* not when your average Cornish person would consider it a lot more sensible to, well, *put some shoes on*.

Walking around with no shoes on may, momentarily, make you feel as if you're in a hot country, but in most hot countries the last thing you'd do is walk around with bare feet, for fear of stepping on something nasty. During my time in Africa I was constantly impressed by what the locals were prepared to wear on their feet, rather than go barefoot. Usually it was something along the lines of an old pair of plimsolls with no laces, but often you saw shoes made from recycled car tyres (basically a piece of tyre cut to the shape of your foot, with a rough strap). I spent three days and nights on a sweltering game count, camping in the Zimbabwean bush with a chap whose feet rattled around, sockless, in a pair of wellies at least two sizes too big for him. He was pretty proud of those wellies. There was no way he was going to walk anywhere with nothing on his feet.

Now, at this time of year, hopefully the weather is defying the memory of the three previous awful spring/summers, and warming up a bit. Great. It's perfectly understandable that we all want to embrace the arrival of the best months of the year. But think twice. It is May. Chances are it's still quite cold. No normal person would take his/her shoes and socks off. Yet I guarantee people will be doing it, thinking it makes them look Cornish. Just keep an eye out. You'll see them.

But don't get me wrong. On the beach, when it's hot, great. Who wouldn't? But be careful. Even in the middle of summer how many of us have regretted leaving our flip flops in the car as we embark on the 300 yard walk to the beach, picking our way through the broken glass, doggie dirt and plastic drink bottle caps?

Possibly the best place to observe this madness is the supermarket at around 5pm on an August Bank Holiday weekend. A young person, probably, giddy on the fact that it's been a bit sunny, understandably keen to embrace the summer lifestyle whilst prolonging their recently ended Australian gap year before returning to some dreadful, grey University somewhere in the Midlands. But the Bohemian image is invariably betrayed either by the scarlet sunburn (if there's been sun) or the conspicuously white feet (if there hasn't). That and the fact that they'll soon be in a state of considerable discomfort as they hurriedly rummage in the frozen food section, whilst simultaneously acquiring a disproportionate fascination with the rotisserie chickens.

Please, don't do it. You're not fooling anyone.

Salad garnish

2006

S o Truro's won an award for being 'Best Food Town in the West Country'. I couldn't quite believe it when I heard. I mean, there's no denying Truro's changed, probably more than anywhere in Cornwall (well, apart from a certain clay pit near St Austell, obviously), but can it really be that my home town, which I've always considered fairly unremarkable on the quality nosh stakes, is now scooping awards?

Analysing the list of fine emporiums and producers to which the esteemed judges had been led, I see that an amazing thing has happened in Truro while I wasn't looking. Virtually all these places weren't there a few years ago. I hadn't really noticed the change, on account of the fact that old Truronians like myself have long since been driven from town by the parking situation, the Treliske/Threemilestone planning mess, and the slow but steady annihilation of small businesses. The latest to go is the lovely Vages jewellers, closing down in the same month that Tesco announces they are about to start selling diamond rings.

So as hordes of discerning diners now rush to Truro from far and wide to snaffle Tuscan tapenade and Cornish asparagus, and plaques go up heralding the city's prestigious new food award, it occurred to me that this really is something to celebrate. Not only because of the gourmet grub, but because this represents the albeit discreet resurgence of the little person. Whether it's a juice bar or a modest microbrewery, these are, by and large, small, one-off businesses. And that is a rare thing these days.

But there's a more important reason to rejoice in this culinary renaissance. Because regardless of all the *Michelin*-starred chefs dotted all over Cornwall, and the commendable upward trend in the availability of fresh, local food, it's a sad fact that below the very top-notch restaurants, there are still some very disappointing meals out there. I went to an award-winning pub recently and ordered the tempting-sounding plaice special at £14. It turned out to be frozen plaice in breadcrumbs with oven chips and vegetables out of a freezer packet. I wouldn't have paid a fiver in a chip shop for it. It's hard to believe that British cuisine has improved significantly when you droolingly order the luscious-sounding home-made steak and ale pie only to be confronted by a few bits of scrag-end floating in a little earthenware dish of brown gloop, invariably with a featherweight balloon of puff pastry teetering pointlessly on top. Caff food, nothing more.

And nowhere is this sad state of affairs more amply demonstrated than in the shameless and laughable use of that ubiquitous hangover from the sixties, the 'salad garnish'. By which I mean: three slices of pallid, ice-cold, unripe tomato, some shreds of tasteless iceberg lettuce, five wafer thin slices of cucumber, and a pinch of cress. Why oh why would any self-respecting chef think that a nice bit of fish is enhanced by the addition of a bitter tomato ripped prematurely from its vine and imported from Spain in January? Such foul activities belong in the distant past, in a world where concentrated orange juice in a glass with a stem passed for a desirable starter. Too often an expensive meal out becomes like a trip into that recent TV cop show where the chap goes back in time to 1973, and everything is brown and tasteless and spaghetti bolognese was new-fangled foreign food not to be trusted and the Galloping Gourmet was a pretty racy fellow.

So whether it's the latest organic scented truffle boutique opening in Truro, or a top restaurant endorsed by an A-list celebrity in Newquay, let's celebrate, because it can only improve things. Next time we're in Truro, after we've fought our way through the ever-increasing roundabouts and American retail strip development at Treliske, queued for an hour and fumbled to find the right change for an overpriced parking space, and dashed across the wind tunnel wilderness that is Lemon Quay precinct, (avoiding speeding buses, boy racers and tumbleweed of course), let's all raise a tall skinny macchiato to this gastronomic metamorphosis.

On the rocks

2013

Maybe you're a bit like me. Picture the scene: you're on the beach, midwinter, the tide's out and you're having a bit of a clamber on the rocks. You peer into the odd rockpool, hoping to spot a startled goby as it dashes for cover. You're vaguely aware that you're in someone else's territory, that any creature or plant you see in a pool, or clinging to an exposed rock, will be breathing a sigh of relief in a few hours' time when this temporary world will be transformed by gazillions of cubic metres of water into somewhere very different.

But that's about it. I tend not to give much more thought to this natural world that's been temporarily revealed. I'm usually much more concerned with where I'm putting my feet, or rather, where my two five-year-olds are putting theirs.

On account of those increasingly inquisitive boys, I'm going on these rocky sojourns more frequently, and as a result, I've been reading up a bit on the subject. And frankly, I'm finding it all a bit, well, mind blowing. It's unbelievable what's going on among the rocks, just as soon as it's all covered in a bit of water! How I've been underestimating all these apparently mundane little creatures all this time.

A great example is barnacles. Boring, right? No! These little guys are amazing! I'd long dismissed them as tiny, dead-looking shelly things that may or may not have harboured something living at some point. But I just needed to take a closer look. When submerged, they've got these beautiful feathery appendages that then methodically sweep microscopic food particles from the water. Watch a bit of footage of this and you'll immediately see that the humble barnacle is a beautiful, busy little animal.

Ever wondered why there are always so many? It's called "swamping". They're so vulnerable to predators that by gathering in vast groups they increase the chances of at least a few surviving. A classic example of 'taking one for the team'. Most interestingly of all, they have the longest penis in the animal kingdom. Yes, really. Up to eight times the size of their own body. Eight times. We're seeing barnacles in a whole new light now aren't we? And once used, it drops off. Talk about giving with one hand and taking away with the other.

OK, enough about barnacles. What about those little beadlet anemones? We've all seen these squidgy, brown jelly blobs when the tide's out. Lots of fun to squeeze and squirt, especially after saying to your friend, "Hey! Come and look at this! You've got to get really close!" Oh come on, we've all done it. But as soon as the tide comes in there it is, in a transformed world, a bona-fide, real life, stunning little anemone, complete with dozens of spidery tentacles.

My whole outlook's changed when I'm on the rocks these days. Did you know that limpets move up to six metres all over the rocks to feed? But they only ever move at night, when it's safer, and they always return home to the exact same position on the rock. Who knew limpets were so sweet? Certainly not me.

It's all even more incredible when you consider the infinite number of other creatures that will be appearing in the vicinity just as soon as it becomes an undersea world again. Perhaps I'm preaching to the converted, in which case I apologise. But it's all come as a bit of a shock to me. Like a lot of things in this world (things we see, people we meet, places we go, things we do…), if we bother to scratch the surface, we are often agreeably surprised. Amazed even. I don't do that nearly often enough.

I used to look at mussels and see white wine and garlic. Not any more.

Lion King raffle

2015

Wow. My family and I just returned from London, where we went to see *The Lion King*. Nothing had prepared me for how good that show would be. Oh sure, I knew that it was the highest grossing stage show of all time. But the Bee Gees are the fifth most successful musical act of all time (or something), and I can't stand them. So I wasn't entirely convinced.

I'd been aware that *The Lion King* had ground-breaking costuming/puppetry, enabling athletic actors to 'become' giraffes, hyenas and elephants on a perfectly realised African savannah. But I didn't realise how truly ambitious, and innovative, and, well, *emotive* it was going to be. It was easily the most expensive show I've ever been to. And yet it was probably the best value. My Cornish seven-year-olds sat with my wife and I, wide-eyed. They were literally on the edge of their seat throughout.

Three weeks earlier, in Cornwall, I'd seen a show that was, to say the least, very different. My twin boys shared the role of Michael in our local Am-Dram group's production of *Peter Pan Junior* in our beachside village hall. It was performed by a cast whose oldest member was sixteen, and directed by an eighteen-year-old. Hmm, local kids in a village hall, I thought. I was fairly convinced that this was going to be a low-key affair – a bunch of children having 'a bit of a go' – a lot of fluffing of lines, and general gurning at friends and family in the audience.

And yet on opening night, the whole thing ran smoothly. More than that, the cast took it in their stride, and the audience loved it. You could see the performers relaxing into their roles, and gaining in confidence with every show. Sure, some lines were mumbled, and the odd cue was missed. But such moments paled in comparison to what these kids had achieved, through hard work and dedication.

So, two shows, at opposite ends of the scale. I wouldn't have missed either of them for anything. In the theatrical capital of the world, we'd seen a production at the very top of its game. Since it started in 1999, *The Lion King* has apparently so far drawn a UK audience of 12 million. And counting. By contrast, down here in the deepest west country, *Peter Pan Junior* was a show staged by amateur kids, pulling in an audience, over its four performances, of a few hundred. The two experiences couldn't have been more different. I've written before about how the little things can be every bit as affecting as the more obvious ones; how swimming with dolphins in some exotic location can be just as wonderful as seeing a lone grey seal bob up next to you when you're surfing at Godrevy. It's not about the scale. It's about how they make you feel.

In London you could go and see something different every night for the rest of your life. But while that probably can't be said for Cornwall, I'm constantly surprised by how much there is going on down here. World class theatre certainly isn't the preserve of our capital. Only last summer, Kneehigh's *946*, staged in their inspiring *Asylum* space at Heligan, was as good as anything I've seen them do. It was as good as anything I've seen *anyone* do.

As I sat there in my plush seat at the *Lyceum* during *The Lion King*'s interval, I reflected on my boys' village hall show, and it made me think. I remembered the decade and a half I spent living in London, and marvelled at the amazing range of opportunities constantly available to me in that metropolis. I found myself comparing it with the downsized, bucolic Cornish life my family and I have chosen for ourselves. And just as the second half was about to start, my son Ben put it all into very sharp focus. He turned to me, and urgently exclaimed: "Daddy! They forgot to do the raffle!"

Self-doubt

2013

Gosh, I'm nervous now.

It's my book, *Notes from a Cornish Shed*, which came out last month. It's not that it's my first book – I had a children's book published six years ago. No, I'm nervous because I'm having self-doubts about my, er, *Cornishness*. You know, my *credibility* as a Cornishman. While I've never exactly claimed to represent Cornwall or the Cornish in any way, I do like to think I've got a half decent grip on things around here. I can at least speak with a modicum of authority when I take pen in hand to fill this back page every month. But I'm very aware that there are plenty of people out there who could validly claim more legitimate Cornish credentials than me.

That said, I was born here, and so were my folks, and most of my grandparents. There, see, I'm doing it now, trying to defend my honour, fight my corner, prove I'm *proper Cornish*. Which I am. Fairly. Oh leave it.

Let's face it, no-one ever wins these arguments. As I've said more than once before on this page, it's all relative. Look at the Rolling Stones. We all know that Mick Jagger's as middle class as they come. And yet in the fabulous 'Jumping Jack Flash' he sounded as if he'd just crawled out of a Louisiana swamp, drawlin' on about being 'baaaaawn' in a hurricane and raised by an old toothless hag. We didn't care that it was faintly ridiculous, because the Stones were brilliant, and they played with convincing authority. Besides, who would have listened to Jagger singing the rather more truthful "*I grew up in Kent and went on to study Business at the London School of Economics!*" I think I speak for all of us when I say that nobody wants to hear that.

Under close scrutiny, some of the most unlikely characters come into question. Remember the Proclaimers? You know, those lovable brothers who belted out such classics as 'I'm gonna be 500 Miles' and 'Letter from America' in such endearingly broad Scottish dialect that we could barely understand a word. They're as Scottish as a deep-fried Mars Bar in a kilt, right? They are so ridiculously, quintessentially *Scottish* that you'd be surprised to hear that they ever set foot south of the border until they were compelled to perform on Top of the Pops in the late eighties, probably against their will. And yet, incredibly, they spent a good two years of their youth living in, of all places, Cornwall! I could hardly believe this myself, but my next door neighbour taught them to play the guitar, so I have it on good authority.

The Proclaimers, living in Cornwall. Who'd have thought. It's preposterous, like discovering David Cameron used to climb out of his Eton dorm window every night and pop down the Working Men's Club to work as a pool hustler. Which I'm fairly sure he didn't. So it strikes me that even if the Proclaimers spent a mere month of their youth outside Scotland, I could justifiably argue that I'm more Cornish than they are Scottish. After all, I never spent any of my youth at all outside Cornwall.

Therefore I hope that you can forgive me if I don't have much of an accent these days, and if your Cornish bloodline is less tainted than mine. I'm still pretty Cornish. I can still do a beauty accent when required, and I can remember Cornwall in the sixties and seventies, when it only ever seemed to cost a few pence to park by the beach (and you got let off if you were a local). I can remember when Truro had half day closing on a Thursday, and I'd cycle to school round a deserted Trafalgar roundabout(!). That's got to count for something.

OK, I've presented my case. I now throw myself upon the mercy of the court.

April Fool

2012

T he thought of April makes us smile like no other month. It's not just that winter has ended (we hope), and we've got it all ahead of us. It's because the first day of April is unique. Oh come on, April Fool's Day is always a bit of fun, isn't it?

There are numerous explanations for the historical origin of this peculiar day, but I don't think anyone's really that interested. We're much more interested in the silliness of it. Probably the most famous April Fool's hoax in this country (and, as far as I'm concerned, never bettered) was the 1957 *Panorama* spoof documentary about the bumper Swiss spaghetti crop, complete with footage of Swiss peasants pulling strands of spaghetti out of trees on the spaghetti plantation. Absolutely brilliant.

There have been numerous other high-profile April Fool's hoaxes over the years, including the invention of the Burger King left-handed burger, Richard Nixon re-running for American president (using the slogan "I didn't do anything wrong, and I won't do it again"), Tesco's whistling carrots, and Patrick Moore announcing that, due to Pluto passing behind Jupiter, there would be a brief reduction in the earth's gravity, resulting in people experiencing a momentary floating sensation. Most shocking of all for Radio 4 listeners was the announcement in 2004 that *The Archers* theme tune was to be scrapped in favour of a more modern electronic version by Brian Eno.

Great stuff. But of course, most of us usually experience April Fool's japery closer to home. Often it's just someone telling us something silly. But a well-placed personal April Fool's gag can be a delight. Last year on April 1, I received an email with 'Early eggs' written in the subject box. It read, '*My home-made hedgehog box has been appreciated by the pair of garden residents who have spent the winter warmly ensconced in it. Yesterday I looked in to see how they were getting on and was surprised to find eggs already. I've never found eggs this early before. Can anyone tell me if this is a record for the UK?*'

Attached were two photos of hedgehogs in the box, and one with a little cluster of tiny eggs in their place. It couldn't have looked more convincing. With hazy memories of bizarre Australian fauna like the spiny echidna, I have to admit that for a split second I was taken in. *Monotremes*, I think the word is: egg-laying mammals. My humour hackles were up as soon as I noticed that the email was from an old friend, Bob Rundle of Camborne (notable wit, and a man whose sense of humour is exceeded only by his uncontrollable appetite for mischief). But if I hadn't had my wits about me, I may have been seriously duped.

The other April Fool's jape I remember from last year was in the papers, brought to my attention by a regular *Backalong* reader. A holidaymaker in Ilfracombe was so appalled and offended by the sight and smell of 12 crates of dead fish stacked on the harbour wall that he complained to the harbour master, and then the local press. He was quoted saying: "The ship was just sat there not doing anything, and there were 12 crates of dead crabs and fish just lying there covered in flies...It's not the sort of thing that you want to see on holiday, there was a real stench."

As April Fool's pranks go, it was good, but I have to say, ridiculously far-fetched. An actual person would never be that daft. And even if they were, they wouldn't draw attention to it with all that publicity, and deliberately make themselves a laughing stock. So it really wasn't as well thought through as Bob's hedgehog eggs. And nowhere near the spaghetti trees.

Wait a minute, what's that you say? It wasn't an April Fool's prank at all? It actually happened, last September? He was a real person, and he really did go to the press to complain that there were some fish in crates on a harbour wall, which smelt? Of fish?

Nah, I don't believe you. That would never happen in real life.

eBooks

2014

Oh joy. Book lovers, we can all breathe. It's going to be OK. For the past few years we've been quaking in our boots, afeared that the 'eBook' is taking over the world, that any day now the very last bookshop will close its doors as the very last person declares they'd rather fiddle about with a little hand-held electronic device than thumb through a lovely, fragrant, tactile, good, old-fashioned *book*.

But no. Recent figures have stated that in the first half of 2014, eBooks only accounted for 23% of 'book' sales, whereas hardcovers made up 25%, and paperbacks a whopping 42%. Now, although 23% still sounds quite significant, it's nowhere near as bad as the apocalyptic predictions about the death of books just a few years ago. We were supposed to have been overrun by device-wielding geeks by now. Which of course we *have* been, watching their HD movies on their smart phones, and sharing interminable photographs of their breakfast with each other. But crucially, as far as ingesting a novel, or encyclopedia, or textbook is concerned, those of us who prefer the traditional format appear to still be in the majority. The printed book is not yet a laughable, quaint museum piece. When my anthology of this column was published just over a year ago, how I agonised over the various formatting options.

An eBook was made available, but how many copies has it sold? I don't even know, but it can certainly be accurately described as a *handful*. In the meantime, I'm very pleased to report that the paperback version moved swiftly to a second edition. Maybe that's got more to do with my readership demographic than any global trend, but it still gives me a warm glow.

So, has the revolution been cancelled, or has it merely slowed down a little? Well at the very least, the two can hopefully now sit comfortably side by side. The eBook is, I admit, an amazing thing. I'm still getting my head round the concept of having an entire library constantly available in your pocket. And they've become indispensable for readers with poor eyesight, or limited storage space (either at home, or when travelling). Not forgetting the geeks, who supposedly prefer to live in houses devoid of possessions (plenty of room for limited edition Battlestar Galactica figurines of course, and tellies the size of a goal mouth, but no room for books).

I don't know if I'll ever work up any enthusiasm for eBooks though. As far as I'm concerned, my house will always be full of books. I don't even quite know why. They're everywhere: the illustrated bird books crammed into the little alcove going up the stairs, the shelf full of Winston Grahams (*Poldark* mostly, with my wife's *Demelza* collection all up one end). Shelves packed with novels in pretty much every room. There are plenty we'll probably never open again, but at least they're there if we ever feel the need. It's not about the practicality anyway – it's more a love thing, rather like my record collection, which I don't actually dip into very often. But that's not the point.

I think I'm probably more sentimental than most. I did work in illustrated book publishing throughout the eighties and nineties, and therefore remember the good old days of paste-up, and casting-off text, and marking up manuscript for the typesetter. I can tell you the difference between a pica em and an en. I loved all that. But it all seems like language from the Victorian era now, not the tail end of the 20th century.

Luddites like me won't be around forever. The book will be killed off by the eBook eventually. Or by something even cleverer, probably. But books have been around a while – we've had the printing press for over five hundred years, so I reckon it's going to take time. A good friend of mine summed it up best: 'eBooks are all very well, but they're fundamentally flawed on two counts: they don't smell the same, and you can't read them in the bath.'

Summer 2014

2014

The weather, that last resort of the conversationally challenged, is a subject I normally try to avoid here on the back page. But I feel I have to say something.

It's April. At last. That time of year when we dare to look ahead, and think about what the summer might hold. And this year the sense of apprehension in the air is keener than ever, because that must have been the worst winter any of us can recall. Not the coldest, maybe, but utterly relentless.

It started as something of a novelty. Remember that twinge of excitement we all used to get when an onshore gale combined with a spring tide? How I used to love seeing Norman Garstin's painting, *The rain it raineth every day*, come to life on the Penzance prom. And how we used to marvel at photos of Porthleven with the sea spray lashing the harbour wall. Many is the time I've stood in Perranporth to enjoy the surreal thrill of watching as the waves, normally so far away, dare to venture briefly onto the beachfront car park. We all used to do it.

But not any more. The fun's over. This is serious. People's lives have been ruined. The novelty's gone, because it's now commonplace, and ghastly, and not fun at all. The flooding's wrecked businesses, homes and lives, all over the country.

Cornwall suffered in ways we couldn't possibly have predicted this time last year, leaving many to re-evaluate the desirability of a sea view. The damage is unprecedented. And now that the drama's ended, there are the repercussions. The expense of it all. The insurance wrangles. It is all just awful.

So weather-wise, we really need a bit of good news, don't we? Just a little something. Normally in April we're all bracing ourselves to be beaten into submission, again, by another promising summer turning out to be a damp squib. But that's not going to happen this year. It can't, for two reasons: *a)* because we need it so badly, after what we've just been through, and *b)* because last summer was nothing short of wonderful.

I don't know about you, but last summer has got my hopes up. I want more. Dare we hope that it could happen again? It was just so mind-blowingly good. It was a summer so far removed from the depressing, grey anticlimaxes of the previous six years that it made Cornwall feel like a different place entirely. For me, it was a case of good timing too, because at five-and-a-half, my twin boys just couldn't get enough of the sea, throwing themselves into it with abandon, and embracing the thrill of catching waves unaided. I lost count of the number of times we'd go straight from school to the beach, clutching belly boards and bags, but blissfully unencumbered with the usual beach paraphernalia (the contingency layers, the waterproofs, the windbreaks...). With each visit, we'd find ourselves jettisoning another item. By mid-August the sea had warmed up so much that I'd given up even putting a wetsuit on. Friends would drift by, and sometimes we'd end up in our local beach bar for an early tea. On leaving, the beach would still be warm and welcoming, so we'd stay another hour or two. Maybe even to watch the sunset.

For this is how it's supposed to be – how it is in Cornwall-based novels, and fantasies, and our childhood memories. What we all want. No need to grin and bear it, make the best of things, and pretend you're not freezing, and disappointed, and getting quite bitter about it all. This was a Cornish summer when I even stopped checking the met office online weather forecast before leaving the house. Cornwall as we all so desperately want it to be, but feel constantly aggrieved that it ain't ever so.

Could it happen again? I mean it couldn't, could it? Not two years running. Surely. And if it does, I wonder how long will it be 'til they start talking about droughts and hosepipe bans?

New Clarrie

2015

A couple of years ago I was washing up with my wife, listening to *The Archers*, like you do, when our jaws simultaneously dropped. "They've changed Clarrie!" cried the missus. She was right. Clarrie Grundy, a character for whom the adjective 'long suffering' seems woefully inadequate, and one of the least irritating of the *Archers* cast, was being voiced by a new actress. "No!" I replied, "How could they! It's just not the same!" Of course, it had happened before – we'd only just adjusted to the new Hayley. But a new Clarrie Grundy was really going to take some getting used to.

And then I read a piece in the paper. The imposter who'd taken over was none other than Heather Bell, the actress who'd voiced the original Clarrie, 36 years ago! This new woman was actually the real deal – she'd practically invented Clarrie Grundy. The Clarrie we'd grown to love in the past twenty or so years was the actual interloper, having done the show for a mere two and a half decades.

This sort of thing happens a lot. You complain about something changing, only to discover that it's actually only reverted back to how it was in the first place, when none of us were complaining at all. There should be a word for it. There may well be one, for all I know.

Something similar happened with our local post office. A few years ago, there was hell up when we started hearing about closures nationwide, and my village was no exception. And then we heard about the plan to cram our little post office into the shop next door. The concept seemed so flawed and unthinkable that it barely registered with me as a viable option. I thought ahead to a nightmarish scenario in early December as, laden with parcels, I'd be queuing at the crowded counter, jostling for elbow room with Haribo-nauseated kids and confused old ladies. What a bun fight this was going to be.

And then someone reminded me that originally the post office was contained within the village shop. Oh, so this was all perfectly normal! In fact it was the sort of setup from the olden days to which we all hark back, longingly. And guess what. It turned out all right. Our new facility does most things the old post office did, and is open longer hours. It's a bit crowded at times, but I'd rather have it crowded than not there at all.

I've got one more example of this sort of thing, and you'll be pleased to hear this one's *Poldark*-related (seeing as how we're all now pining badly for Ross's hairy chest, or Demelza's tousled tresses, or, in some cases, both. I'm planning to bring the subject of *Poldark* up at any available opportunity as therapy). In the very first episode of the recent series, there was a rather incongruous, violent fight scene towards the end, in which Demelza's old man goes at it with Ross, while his Illogan henchmen take on trusty villagers Zacky, Jim, Mark etc. in an equally bloody incident. It jarred, in what had been an otherwise enjoyable first episode. I didn't remember such scenes from the book, nor from the original series. "I don't remember this!" I shouted at the telly. Straight back to the book I went, keen to prove how badly they'd veered away from the literature in the pursuit of some crowd-pleasing violence. But sure enough there it was, on page 109 of *Ross Poldark*, unpleasant fisticuffs all round. It was extremely accurately adapted, as was the rest of the series, as it turned out.

So, another lesson learned. We all like to complain, from time to time, that things are changing for the worse. I certainly do. But it's surprising how often we find we're actually finding fault where there is none, and that it's our own assumptions that we should be questioning. Er, if you see what I mean. See, there definitely should be a word for it.

Wet Nurse

2016

W ell, I've covered a fair few subjects on this page in the past, but here's one I bet you never thought you'd hear: wet nurses.

Yes, as I write, there's a prominent local news story about a young mum who was recently admitted to Treliske Hospital (sorry, the *Royal Cornwall* Hospital – I'll never get used to it). She was concerned about her 11-month-old son being unable to breastfeed while she was too ill. So she put out a message on social media, asking for volunteer wet nurses! Incredibly, around a thousand people came forward, and a team of five CRB-checked women organised themselves to feed the little boy until his mum was well enough to resume. It was quite a story. In fact I just listened to it on Radio 4's *PM programme*, no less, with the dramatic introduction: '*Would you let a stranger breastfeed your baby?*' The mum was interviewed, and also a very eloquent, Truro-based volunteer 'wet nurse'. At the end of the chat, I was left thinking 'OK, that all sounds very sensible'.

What's more, I felt a distinct sense of pride that this had all taken place here in Cornwall. You could argue that a story about wet nursing in 21st century Cornwall is an obvious open invitation for yet more cheap mockery of us as an olde worlde rural backwater. But I like to think it shows us as a bit alternative – a place where we're keen to think outside the box. I'd go as far as to say that it made me feel proud to be Cornish. That interview wasn't a million miles away from when Newlyn's Jack Nowell hit Robbie Henshaw like a freight train in England's Six Nations match against Ireland, crucially denying him a try. Watching that gave me a patriotic Cornish warm glow too (even if Jack was playing for *England*).

But I digress. You're probably guessing that I'm a fan of breastfeeding. You'd be right, in as much as a person with neither paediatric qualifications nor breasts can be. But I am nevertheless proud to say that I'm a parent of twins, neither of whom ever went near formula milk. Obviously one has to put this down to 99.9% input from my wife (a passionate advocate of the 'breast is best' mantra), but I'm very proud of the 0.1% I put in. You know, in a supportive role.

You often hear negative publicity about this most natural of activities, from all sorts of angles. There are those who believe you shouldn't be allowed to do it in public, no matter how discreetly, and there are those who think it's not really necessary at all, because we've transcended the need for it with science. But breastfeeding's huge range of health benefits can't be ignored, from the big reduction in many types of infection to the boost in immunity. Not to mention the estimated £500 you can save on all that kitchen-cluttering, sterilising paraphernalia.

I'm sure the poorly mum wasn't planning on getting national media attention when she appealed for volunteers that day, but I reckon her actions may have done more to promote a positive image of breastfeeding than all the earnest literature the NHS puts out in a year.

People have legitimately questioned the wisdom of giving a stranger (let alone five of them) responsibility for your child, as well as the fact that there was no medical screening for any of the wet nurses (let's see: alcohol intake....HIV status...one of the ladies was from Devon for heaven's sake). These are surely valid arguments (not the Devon one – that was a joke). But I'm fairly confident that she wanted nothing more than her son's nutritional and emotional welfare to be compromised as little as possible, and this was her instinctive solution. Above all, I think it's so inspiring that all those volunteers spontaneously stepped forward, keen to do their bit, and fly the flag for something they passionately believe in. But then, that's Cornwall for you.

Gosh, that was all a bit intense. Next month: *Poldark*. Or pasties. Or something.

Half way

2017

Goodness me – I just realised that with the recent conclusion of series three of *Poldark*, we've covered six out of Winston Graham's twelve books. Half way! Incredibly, this means that we're already almost at the point where the original seventies TV series ended. Just like that!

With Ross now fully solvent, any mining-related plot shenanigans have been put on the backburner, paving the way for a battalion of new characters who, in different ways, are all ramping up the Poldark/Warleggan conflict: the attractive Carne boys, Elizabeth's attractive cousins, attractive Hugh Armitage…

Ah, but then there's Reverend Osborne Whitworth – a man so awful that if the *Oxford Illustrated Dictionary* needed to succinctly define the word *repugnant,* they'd only need to print a picture of the man's snooty, lascivious visage. As far as vile literary characters go, Whitworth really has to be *up there.* Now, most of us have quickly become acclimatised to all these new actors in the familiar *Poldark* roles (even Jud and Prudie – I didn't think that was possible!), but I'd really been struggling to imagine Osborne Whitworth played by anyone other than Christopher Biggins. Biggins did such a great job as the loathsome fop that when I spotted the actual actor walking past a Covent Garden pub in the mid-eighties, just the sight of him still sent a shiver of loathing up my spine (fortunately he managed to shake off the legacy of Whitworth as Biggins has become something of a national treasure these days).

When the all-new Osborne Whitworth first appeared on our screens, my wife (a proper Poldark purist – not a fairweather fan like me) thought that the new actor didn't look right at all. Not like Biggins. Not nearly slimy enough. "Oh come on," I said, "You've got to give him a chance. We got over them making Demelza a redhead, *again*, so let's just see". Sure enough, the *Poldark* casting department knew exactly what they were doing. The more acceptable Whitworth seems when we first clap eyes on him, the more shocking his atrocities appear as he reveals the appalling layers beneath. After all, at the beginning he's supposed to be a plausible match for Morwenna. In the book, Winston Graham actually described Whitworth as tall, and 'well-aware of his good looks'.

Of course, there's one Poldark character that stands head and shoulders above everyone. No, not old Abs Turner. Not the feisty, steadfast, natural, sultry, funny, compellingly watchable and achingly beautiful Demelza, with the lustrous hair, and the gorgeous smile (crikey, gave myself away a bit there didn't I? And she can sing. Just saying). Not even Garrick the dog.

You know what I'm going to say don't you? The unrivalled star of the show is of course *Cornwall*. Or, more specifically, the *Cornish coastline*. Oh, the endlessly sweeping aerial footage. Oh, the constant walking/running/galloping across deserted beaches for no apparent reason. I thought it was gratuitous in the seventies, but they've really upped their game now. I've heard of a sizeable audience demographic of *Poldark* viewers who are just that: *viewers*. They watch it with the sound down.

Not that I'm complaining – perhaps I'm sounding cynical because I'm lucky enough to have that scenery a ten minute walk from my front door. Just like *Doc Martin* (in which every time the good doctor makes a home visit, there's always a stunning sea view out of the patient's bedroom window), the sea is right there, in your face, at every conceivable opportunity. No matter how much of a hurry Ross is in, he still, ludicrously, gallops for miles teetering atop the cliff's edge. I'm sure I even spotted a big granite signpost on the cliff top directing him to Falmouth, on the opposite coast, pointing along the coastline. I ask you. You'd think if Ross could work out how to get to Dwight Enys's jail somewhere in deepest Brittany in the dark using a map drawn by a five-year-old, he'd have worked out that you're going to get to Falmouth quicker if you turn ninety degrees and travel, well, *inland*.

Cornwall, UK

2014

L ike many, I've never thought of Cornwall as being part of England. Don't get me wrong – I know that we are, at least officially, in England. Yet in my 51 years as a Cornish-person, I have never, to my knowledge, ever referred to 'Cornwall, England'. It's 'Cornwall, UK', and always has been. I'm pretty sure that my dad taught me that when I was a boy, just as I've found myself explaining it to my boys. I know countless others who feel the same way. When I've mentioned it to people over the years, for every one person who calmly agrees, there have probably been three who openly laugh in my face at what they perceive to be small-minded, naïve parochialism.

It's not easy to define why we don't feel like just another English county; why so many of us have always felt that we are a separate country, and yet not quite one. I think it has to do with a very broad range of exclusive factors: the fact that we're a geographical extremity, like Scotland and Wales, our history as a Celtic nation, the unique landscape, our industrial heritage, our dialect, our language... It's a feeling. It's just inside us.

When the news broke that we were to be recognised as a national minority, it was the culmination of a lot of hard work by people who feel the same way I do, but more strongly. While they were (I hope) patting themselves on the back and toasting their success with a pint of Betty Stogs, most of us were trying to get our heads round what this was actually going to mean, in real terms. Could it be that we were actually a *country* now, like Wales – truly recognised as a Celtic nation? Could that really be possible? How would we be treated now? Was there going to be any money in it? What was going to change? Or was it nothing more than a cynical attempt by the Lib Dems to claw back some of their many lost Cornish votes?

Straightaway all over the media there was speculation about who exactly qualified. They kept going on about 'Cornish people' and 'The Cornish', but *how* Cornish did you have to be to be included? Born here? Parents born here? Grandparents? Two out of four grandparents? Great, great, great grandparents? Many commentators suggested that as long as you live in Cornwall, you are Cornish. To which I saw one blogger reply that if he moves to Holland, can he call then himself a Dutchman the next day? Cornish comedian Ed Rowe, The Kernow King, put his finger on it (as with most comedians his tongue-in-cheek comedy persona belies a sharp mind): "It's not about genetics, it's simply about 'living and loving being in Cornwall'".

By the next day there was a surprising amount of negativity in the media. "Am I alone in finding this sort of...*sad*?" was one pitying comment on *The Guardian*'s website. A *Daily Mail* columnist referred to it as a 'shameful stunt' and made a (not altogether serious I suspect) play for his home county of Essex to be given the same status. *The Independent* went as far as inviting representatives from every English county to write a piece in support of his or her own county's suitability.

Coincidentally, a few weeks before the momentous news, we'd been the butt of the joke on primetime BBC2 comedy *W1A*, in which Hugh Bonneville as BBC Head of Values, had to deal with the fictitious leader of Mebyon Kernow who was aggrieved at the BBC's supposed anti-Cornish bias. Of course the actor presented us with the usual Bristol/Norfolk hybrid bumpkin accent. We've always been a soft target for such attacks, we Cornish. It's partly because we're so laid-back. The fact is that to a large number of people upcountry we're the land of country bumpkins, piskies, pasties, clotted cream and bucket-and-spade holidays. And little more.

I'd be the first to admit that some of the more obvious trappings of our Cornishness are open to debate. Our tartan was invented in the sixties. No-one *really* knows where or when the flag of St Piran originated. St Piran isn't even the patron saint of Cornwall, but of tin miners, and was Irish (somehow he managed to elbow St Michael out of the way, possibly due to the fact that the latter's name conjures up visions of twin packs of pants). There are still only a few hundred people fluent in Cornish, and some of our 'traditional' festivals have only really been revived comparatively recently.

But that is actually the point. In recent years there's been an unprecedented groundswell of pride in Cornwall, leading to renewed interest in our festivals, our language, and all things Cornish. When I was a kid nobody spoke Kernewek. We were all taught that Dolly Pentreath died in 1777, and that she was the last fluent speaker, and that was about it. But in 2002, Cornish became recognised as a minority language by the UK government under the European Charter for Regional or Minority Languages. It may be true that not many people are fluent, but small phrases are popping up in everyday life (the *Radio Cornwall* breakfast show presenter's *myttin da* greeting every morning, *Facebook* users all wishing each other 'Happy St Piran's Day' in Cornish...). St Piran's Day used to go unnoticed, recognised only by a small minority, but it's now celebrated in different ways by communities all over Cornwall. A few years ago you were more likely to celebrate St Patrick's Day than St Piran's. Not now. We're only one step away from St Piran's Day becoming a Bank Holiday.

There are so many factors contributing to our renewed awareness of our culture. Choughs returned here in 2001, and have been slowly re-colonizing our coastline ever since. Just a few years ago, the Kernow King hilariously latched onto some of the quirky little things about being Cornish, and thus subversively reminded us that it is a thing to be cherished and celebrated. He now has tens of thousands of fans.

This place is buzzing. But the fact is, we Cornish don't care that much about what people think of us. Having national minority status will doubtless increase our profile and improve our standing and credibility on a bigger stage. That's great. We're still a long way from having a devolved government, but for the time being this feels about right. We've been in on the secret a long time. Now it's just a bit less of a secret.